Kubernetes

Preparing for the CKA and CKAD Certifications

Philippe Martin

Apress®

Kubernetes

Philippe Martin
Gif-sur-Yvette, France

ISBN-13 (pbk): 978-1-4842-6493-5   ISBN-13 (electronic): 978-1-4842-6494-2
https://doi.org/10.1007/978-1-4842-6494-2

Managing Director, Apress Media LLC: Welmoed Spahr
Acquisitions Editor: Spandana Chatterjee
Development Editor: Matthew Moodie
Coordinating Editor: Divya Modi

Cover designed by eStudioCalamar

Cover image designed by Pixabay

Distributed to the book trade worldwide by Springer Science+Business Media New York, 1 New York Plaza, Suite 4600, New York, NY 10004-1562, USA. Phone 1-800-SPRINGER, fax (201) 348-4505, e-mail orders-ny@springer-sbm.com, or visit www.springeronline.com. Apress Media, LLC is a California LLC and the sole member (owner) is Springer Science + Business Media Finance Inc (SSBM Finance Inc). SSBM Finance Inc is a **Delaware** corporation.

For information on translations, please e-mail booktranslations@springernature.com; for reprint, paperback, or audio rights, please e-mail bookpermissions@springernature.com.

Apress titles may be purchased in bulk for academic, corporate, or promotional use. eBook versions and licenses are also available for most titles. For more information, reference our Print and eBook Bulk Sales web page at http://www.apress.com/bulk-sales.

Any source code or other supplementary material referenced by the author in this book is available to readers on GitHub via the book's product page, located at www.apress.com/978-1-4842-6493-5. For more detailed information, please visit http://www.apress.com/source-code.

Printed on acid-free paper

To Mélina and Elsa, my source of truth

Table of Contents

About the Author

 **Philippe Martin** has been working with Kubernetes for three years, first by creating an operator to deploy video CDNs into the cloud and later helping companies deploy their applications into Kubernetes. Philippe passed CKAD certification about a year ago and CKA certification recently.

He has long experience with distributed systems and open source software; he started his career 20 years ago creating thin clients based on the Linux kernel and open source components.

Philippe is active in the development of the Kubernetes community, especially its documentation, and participates in the translation of the official documentation in French, has edited two reference books about Kubernetes API and kubectl, and is responsible for French translation of the Kubernetes Dashboard.

About the Technical Reviewer

Prasanth Sahoo is a thought leader, an adjunct professor, a technical speaker, and a full-time practitioner in Blockchain, Cloud, and Scrum working for Tata Consultancy Services. He has implemented solution architectures with automating and orchestrating workloads on cloud service providers like Microsoft Azure and Google Cloud and also led cross-functional teams to achieve their goals using agile methodologies. He is passionate about driving digital technology initiatives by handling various community initiatives through coaching, mentoring, and grooming techniques.

He is a working group member in the Blockchain Council, CryptoCurrency Certification Consortium, Scrum Alliance, Scrum Organization, and International Institute of Business Analysis.

Introduction

Kubernetes is a recent platform, based on more than ten years of experience in cloud computing by big companies like Google, its creator. It is considered complex as it includes all the concepts to run diverse applications in a large variety of environments.

This book, based on the curricula of the two Kubernetes certifications (Application Developer and Administrator), introduces all the concepts and tools necessary to administer a Kubernetes cluster and deploy applications in production.

The target reader for this book is an application developer or a system administrator having a good knowledge in microservice development and deployment.

We are going to assume that you know how to create container images and deploy containers with Docker or Docker Compose and that you have some experience installing and managing Linux servers on virtual machines (VMs).

This book includes 16 chapters. The first three chapters cover the installation of a fresh new cluster, the exploration of its components, and the installation of its CLI. Chapters 4–13 present the main elementary blocks composing an application deployed in Kubernetes and how to make your application configurable, scalable, resilient, and secured. Chapters 14–15 cover the observability of your application and the maintenance of your cluster. The last chapter is a wrap-up of the commands provided by the Kubernetes CLI and its companions:

- Chapter 1 is a walk-through to install a Kubernetes cluster using kubeadm on virtual machines in Google Cloud Platform.

- Chapter 2 explores the components installed during the previous chapter.

- Chapter 3 guides you on how to install the CLI and configure it to access the cluster installed in Chapter 1.

- Chapter 4 explains what the building blocks of a Kubernetes application are, how to partition them using namespaces, and how to decorate them using labels and annotations.

- Chapter 5 describes the principle of controllers, omnipresent in Kubernetes, and details how workload controllers work.

- Chapter 6 enumerates and dives into the possibilities for configuring your applications.

- Chapter 7 explores the ways to scale your workloads manually or automatically.

- Chapter 8 explains how to set up your application to make it self-healing with the help of controllers, probes, and resource limits.

- Chapter 9 explores the different ways to control the schedule of workloads on cluster nodes.

- Chapter 10 explains how workloads are made accessible with services and ingresses.

- Chapter 11 covers the different authentication methods, the RBAC authorization model, security contexts, network policies, and how to secure container images.

- Chapter 12 covers the use of persistent volumes to make your applications stateful.

- Chapter 13 explains the main design patterns for multi-container Pods.

- Chapter 14 shows you the basic possibilities for logging and monitoring.

- Chapter 15 is a walk-through to upgrade your cluster.

- Chapter 16 details the commands available with the kubectl CLI and covers the Helm and Kustomize tools to make the deployment of your applications easier.

- Appendixes detail the curricula for the CKA and CKAD certifications.

CHAPTER 1

Creating a Cluster with kubeadm

In this chapter, you will deploy a Kubernetes cluster on virtual machines (VMs) in Google Cloud.

Provisioning Compute Resources

You will install a single control plane cluster. For this, you will need one virtual machine for the controller and several (here two) virtual machines for the workers.

Full network connectivity among all machines in the cluster is necessary. For this, you will create a Virtual Private Cloud (VPC) that will host the cluster and define a subnet to get addresses for the hosts.

From the Google Cloud Console, create a new project my-project; then, from a local terminal, log in and set the current region, zone, and project (you can also work from the Google Cloud Shell and skip the login step):

```
$ gcloud auth login
[...]
$ gcloud config set compute/region us-west1
Updated property [compute/region].
$ gcloud config set compute/zone us-west1-c
```

© Philippe Martin 2021
P. Martin, *Kubernetes*, https://doi.org/10.1007/978-1-4842-6494-2_1

```
Updated property [compute/zone].
$ gcloud config set project my-project
Updated property [core/project].
```

Create a dedicated Virtual Private Cloud (VPC):

```
$ gcloud compute networks create kubernetes-cluster --subnet-
mode custom
Created [https://www.googleapis.com/compute/v1/projects/my-
project/global/networks/kubernetes-cluster].
```

Create a subnet in the kubernetes-cluster VPC:

```
$ gcloud compute networks subnets create kubernetes \
  --network kubernetes-cluster \
  --range 10.240.0.0/24
Created [https://www.googleapis.com/compute/v1/projects/my-
project/regions/us-west1/subnetworks/kubernetes].
```

Create firewall rules for internal communications:

```
$ gcloud compute firewall-rules create \
  kubernetes-cluster-allow-internal \
  --allow tcp,udp,icmp \
  --network kubernetes-cluster \
  --source-ranges 10.240.0.0/24,10.244.0.0/16
Created [https://www.googleapis.com/compute/v1/projects/my-
project/global/firewalls/kubernetes-cluster-allow-internal].
```

Create firewall rules for external communications:

```
$ gcloud compute firewall-rules create \
  kubernetes-cluster-allow-external \
  --allow tcp:22,tcp:6443,icmp \
```

```
--network kubernetes-cluster \
--source-ranges 0.0.0.0/0
```
Created [https://www.googleapis.com/compute/v1/projects/my-project/global/firewalls/kubernetes-cluster-allow-external].

Reserve a public IP address for the controller:

```
$ gcloud compute addresses create kubernetes-controller \
  --region $(gcloud config get-value compute/region)
```
Created [https://www.googleapis.com/compute/v1/projects/my-project/regions/us-west1/addresses/kubernetes-controller].
```
$ PUBLIC_IP=$(gcloud compute addresses describe kubernetes-controller \
    --region $(gcloud config get-value compute/region) \
    --format 'value(address)')
```

Create a VM for the controller:

```
$ gcloud compute instances create controller \
    --async \
    --boot-disk-size 200GB \
    --can-ip-forward \
    --image-family ubuntu-1804-lts \
    --image-project ubuntu-os-cloud \
    --machine-type n1-standard-1 \
    --private-network-ip 10.240.0.10 \
    --scopes compute-rw,storage-ro,service-management,service-control, logging-write, monitoring \
    --subnet kubernetes \
    --address $PUBLIC_IP
```
Instance creation in progress for [controller]: [...]

Create VMs for the workers:

```
$ for i in 0 1; do \
  gcloud compute instances create worker-${i} \
    --async \
    --boot-disk-size 200GB \
    --can-ip-forward \
    --image-family ubuntu-1804-lts \
    --image-project ubuntu-os-cloud \
    --machine-type n1-standard-1 \
    --private-network-ip 10.240.0.2${i} \
    --scopes compute-rw,storage-ro,service-management,service-
      control,logging-write, monitoring \
    --subnet kubernetes; \
done
Instance creation in progress for [worker-0]: [...]
Instance creation in progress for [worker-1]: [...]
```

Install Docker on the Hosts

Repeat these steps for the controller and each worker.

Connect to the host (here the controller):

```
$ gcloud compute ssh controller
```

Install Docker service:

```
# Install packages to allow apt to use a repository over HTTPS
$ sudo apt-get update && sudo apt-get install -y \
  apt-transport-https ca-certificates curl software-properties-
  common
```

```
# Add Docker's official GPG key
$ curl -fsSL https://download.docker.com/linux/ubuntu/gpg |
sudo apt-key add -

# Add Docker apt repository
$ sudo add-apt-repository \
  "deb [arch=amd64] https://download.docker.com/linux/ubuntu \
  $(lsb_release -cs) \
  stable"

# List available versions of Docker
$ apt-cache madison docker-ce

# Install Docker CE, for example version 5:19.03.12~3-0
$ sudo apt-get update && sudo apt-get install -y \
  docker-ce=5:19.03.12~3-0~ubuntu-bionic \
  docker-ce-cli=5:19.03.12~3-0~ubuntu-bionic

$ sudo apt-mark hold containerd.io docker-ce docker-ce-cli

# Setup daemon
$ cat <<EOF | sudo tee /etc/docker/daemon.json
{
  "exec-opts": ["native.cgroupdriver=systemd"],
  "log-driver": "json-file",
  "log-opts": {
    "max-size": "100m"
  },
  "storage-driver": "overlay2"
}
EOF

$ sudo mkdir -p /etc/systemd/system/docker.service.d
```

```
# Restart docker
$ sudo systemctl daemon-reload
$ sudo systemctl restart docker
$ sudo systemctl enable docker
```

Install kubeadm, kubelet, and kubectl on the Hosts

Repeat these steps for the controller and each worker.

Connect to the host (here the controller):

```
$ gcloud compute ssh controller
```

Install kubelet, kubeadm, and kubectl:

```
# Add GPG key
$ curl -s https://packages.cloud.google.com/apt/doc/apt-key.gpg
| sudo apt-key add -

# Add Kubernetes apt repository
$ cat <<EOF | sudo tee /etc/apt/sources.list.d/kubernetes.list
deb https://apt.kubernetes.io/ kubernetes-xenial main
EOF

# Get Kubernetes apt repository data
$ sudo apt-get update

# List available versions of kubeadm
$ apt-cache madison kubeadm

# Install selected version (here 1.18.6-00)
$ sudo apt-get install -y kubelet=1.18.6-00 kubeadm=1.18.6-00
kubectl=1.18.6-00
$ sudo apt-mark hold kubelet kubeadm kubectl
```

Initialize the Control Plane Node

Run these steps on the controller only.

Initialize the cluster (that should take several minutes):

```
$ gcloud config set compute/zone us-west1-c # or your selected zone
Updated property [compute/zone].
$ KUBERNETES_PUBLIC_ADDRESS=$(gcloud compute instances describe
controller \
  --zone $(gcloud config get-value compute/zone) \
  --format='get(networkInterfaces[0].accessConfigs[0].natIP)')
$ sudo kubeadm init \
  --pod-network-cidr=10.244.0.0/16 \
  --ignore-preflight-errors=NumCPU \
  --apiserver-cert-extra-sans=$KUBERNETES_PUBLIC_ADDRESS
```

At the end of the initialization, a message gives you a command to join the workers to the cluster (a command starting with kubeadm join). Please copy this command for later use.

Save the *kubeconfig* file generated by the installation in your home directory. It will give you *admin* access to the cluster:

```
$ mkdir -p $HOME/.kube
$ sudo cp -i /etc/kubernetes/admin.conf $HOME/.kube/config
$ sudo chown $(id -u):$(id -g) $HOME/.kube/config
$ kubectl get nodes
NAME          STATUS      ROLES     AGE      VERSION
Controller    NotReady    master    1m14s    v1.18.6
```

Install the calico Pod network add-on:

```
$ kubectl apply -f https://docs.projectcalico.org/manifests/
calico.yaml
```

Wait till the end of the installation. All Pods should have a *Running* status:

```
$ kubectl get pods -A
```

When all the Pods are *Running*, the master node should be *Ready*:

```
$ kubectl get nodes
NAME         STATUS  ROLES   AGE     VERSION
Controller   Ready   master  2m23s   v1.18.6
```

Join the Workers

Repeat these steps for each worker.

Run the command you saved after running kubeadm init on the controller:

```
$ sudo kubeadm join 10.240.0.10:6443 --token <token> \
  --discovery-token-ca-cert-hash sha256:<hash>
```

If you didn't save the command, you have to get the token and hash. On the controller, run:

```
$ kubeadm token list
TOKEN                      TTL   EXPIRES
abcdef.ghijklmnopqrstuv    23h   2020-01-19T08:25:27Z
```

Tokens expire after 24 hours. If yours expired, you can create a new one:

8

```
$ kubeadm token create
bcdefg.hijklmnopqrstuvw
```

To obtain the hash value, you can run this command on the controller:

```
$ openssl x509 -pubkey -in /etc/kubernetes/pki/ca.crt | \
    openssl rsa -pubin -outform der 2>/dev/null | \
    openssl dgst -sha256 -hex | sed 's/^.* //'
8cb2de97839780a412b93877f8507ad6c94f73add17d5d7058e91741c9d5ec78
```

CHAPTER 2

Control Plane Components

The Kubernetes control plane is composed of

- The API server kube-apiserver, the front end for the Kubernetes control plane

- The key-value store etcd, the backing store of all cluster data

- The scheduler kube-scheduler, which selects nodes for new Pods to run on

- The Controller Manager kube-controller-manager, which embeds all the controllers, including the *Node controller, Replication controller, Endpoints controller, and Service Account and Token controllers.*

On each node, the components running are

- kubelet, which makes sure the Pods affected to the node are running correctly

- kube-proxy, which maintains network rules on nodes to satisfy the Service demands

© Philippe Martin 2021
P. Martin, *Kubernetes*, https://doi.org/10.1007/978-1-4842-6494-2_2

Explore the Control Plane Services

The kubelet service runs as a Unix service, and its status and logs are accessible by using the traditional systemd command-line tools:

```
$ systemctl status kubelet
[...]
$ journalctl -u kubelet
[...]
```

The other services are running in the Kubernetes cluster and visible in the kube-system namespace. You can get the status by using the kubectl describe command and the logs by using the kubectl logs command:

```
$ kubectl get pods -n kube-system
etcd-controller
kube-apiserver-controller
kube-controller-manager-controller
kube-proxy-123456
kube-proxy-789012
kube-proxy-abcdef
kube-scheduler-controller

$ kubectl describe pods -n kube-system etcd-controller
[...]
$ kubectl logs -n kube-system etcd-controller
[...]
```

You probably wonder what magic makes the Kubernetes control plane run in Kubernetes itself. This is thanks to the Static Pods feature, with which it is possible to give Pod definitions directly to a kubelet service. You can find the manifests of the Pods in the following directory of the controller:

```
$ gcloud compute ssh controller
Welcome to controller
$ ls /etc/kubernetes/manifests/
etcd.yaml
kube-apiserver.yaml
kube-controller-manager.yaml
kube-scheduler.yaml
```

CHAPTER 3

Accessing the Cluster

In the previous chapters, you have installed kubectl on the Kubernetes hosts and used it from these hosts. The usual way of using the kubectl command is to install it on your development machine.

In this chapter, you will see how to install kubectl on your machine and how to configure it to access the cluster you installed in Chapter 1.

Install kubectl on Your dev Machine

Depending on the operating system you are running on your development machine, follow one of these instructions:

Linux

```
$ curl -LO https://storage.googleapis.com/kubernetes-release/
release/v1.18.6/bin/linux/amd64/kubectl
$ chmod +x ./kubectl
$ sudo mv ./kubectl /usr/local/bin/kubectl
# Test it is working correctly
$ kubectl version --client --short
Client Version: v1.18.6
```

© Philippe Martin 2021
P. Martin, *Kubernetes*, https://doi.org/10.1007/978-1-4842-6494-2_3

macOS

```
$ curl -LO https://storage.googleapis.com/kubernetes-release/
release/v1.18.6/bin/darwin/amd64/kubectl
$ chmod +x ./kubectl
$ sudo mv ./kubectl /usr/local/bin/kubectl
# Test it is working correctly
$ kubectl version --client --short
Client Version: v1.18.6
```

Windows

```
$ curl -LO https://storage.googleapis.com/kubernetes-release/
release/v1.18.6/bin/windows/amd64/kubectl.exe
# Move the binary into your PATH,
$ kubectl version --client --short
Client Version: v1.18.6
```

Access the Cluster from the dev Machine

Get the kubeconfig file for the new cluster:

```
$ gcloud compute scp controller:~/.kube/config kubeconfig
```

Update the IP address to access the cluster in the file:

```
$ KUBERNETES_PUBLIC_ADDRESS=$(gcloud compute instances describe
controller \
   --zone $(gcloud config get-value compute/zone) \
   --format='get(networkInterfaces[0].accessConfigs[0].natIP)')
$ sed -i "s/10.240.0.10/$KUBERNETES_PUBLIC_ADDRESS/" kubeconfig
```

If you do not have a kubeconfig file yet, you can copy it in $HOME/.kube/config:

```
$ mv -i kubeconfig $HOME/.kube/config
```

If you already have a kubeconfig file, you can merge this new one with the existing one. First, examine the kubeconfig file:

```
apiVersion: v1
clusters:
- cluster:
    certificate-authority-data: <...>
    server: https://<ip>:6443
  name: kubernetes
contexts:
- context:
    cluster: kubernetes
    user: kubernetes-admin
  name: kubernetes-admin@kubernetes
current-context: kubernetes-admin@kubernetes
kind: Config
preferences: {}
users:
    - name: kubernetes-admin
      user:
        client-certificate-data: <...>
        client-key-data: <...>
```

You can see that this file defines a cluster named kubernetes, a user named kubernetes-admin, and a context kubernetes-admin@kubernetes.

These names are very generic (if you create several clusters with kubeadm, all kubeconfig files will define these elements with the same names). We will first replace them with more specific ones:

```
$ sed -i 's/kubernetes/cka/' kubeconfig
```

Then, we can merge this file with the existing $HOME/.kube/config one:

```
$ KUBECONFIG=$HOME/.kube/config:kubeconfig \
  kubectl config view --merge --flatten > config \
  && mv config $HOME/.kube/config
```

Finally, you can switch the current context to cka-admin@kubernetes:

```
$ kubectl config use-context cka-admin@kubernetes
Switched to context "cka-admin@kubernetes".
```

CHAPTER 4

Kubernetes Resources

Kubernetes works in a declarative way: you create **resources** with the help of the Kubernetes API, these objects are stored in the etcd store, and controllers work to ensure that what you declared in these objects is correctly deployed in your infrastructure.

Most of the resources are composed of three parts: the **metadata**, the **spec**, and the **status**.

The **spec** is the specification **you** provide to the cluster. This is what the controllers will examine to know what to do.

The **status** represents the current status of the resource in the infrastructure, as observed by **controllers**. This is what you will examine to know how the resource is deployed in the infrastructure.

The **metadata** contains other information like the name of the resource, the namespace it belongs to, labels, annotations, and so on.

Namespaces

Some resources (called namespaced resources) belong to a namespace. A namespace is a logical separation, and names of resources must be unique in a namespace.

RBAC authorization uses the namespaces to define authorizations based on the namespace of resources.

© Philippe Martin 2021
P. Martin, *Kubernetes*, https://doi.org/10.1007/978-1-4842-6494-2_4

You can create new namespaces with the command:

```
$ kubectl create namespace my-ns
namespace/my-ns created
```

Then, when running kubectl commands, you can specify the namespace on which the command operates with the flag --namespace, or --all-namespaces (-A for short) to operate in all namespaces.

You can also specify the default namespace you want to work on, with:

```
$ kubectl config set-context \
    --current --namespace=my-ns
Context "minikube" modified.
```

Labels and Selectors

Any number of key-value pairs, named labels, can be attached to any resource. These labels are mainly used by components of Kubernetes and by tools to select resources by attributes (materialized by labels) instead of by name:

- Lots of kubectl commands accept a --selector (-l for short) flag which permits to select resources by labels:

  ```
  $ kubectl get pods -l app=nginx -A
  ```

- Services, which route traffic to Pods, select the Pods with a label selector:

  ```
  apiVersion: v1
  kind: Service
  metadata:
    name: nginx
  ```

```
spec:
  selector:
    # distribute traffic to all pods with this label
    app: nginx
  ports:
  - port: 80
```

- A Deployment, which is responsible for maintaining alive a given number of Pods, uses a label selector to find the Pods it is responsible for (see Chapter 5, section "Pod Controllers"):

```
apiVersion: apps/v1
kind: Deployment
metadata:
  name: nginx
spec:
  selector:
    # the pods managed by the Deployment
    # are the ones with this label
    matchLabels:
      app: nginx
  template:
    metadata:
      # pods created by the Deployment
      # will have this label
      labels:
        app: nginx
    spec:
      containers:
      - image: nginx
        name: nginx
```

- You can select the attributes of the node on which
  you want to deploy a Pod by using label selectors (see
  Chapter 9, section "Using label selectors to schedule
  Pods on specific nodes").

Annotations

Annotations are metadata attached to a resource, generally intended for
tools and Kubernetes extensions, but not yet integrated in the spec part.
You can add annotations to a resource in an imperative way:

```
$ kubectl annotate deployments.apps nginx \
   mytool/mem-size=1G
deployment.apps/nginx annotated
```

or in a declarative way:

```
apiVersion: apps/v1
kind: Deployment
metadata:
  annotations:
    mytool/mem-size: 1G
  name: nginx
[...]
```

CHAPTER 5

The Workloads

The Pod is the masterpiece of the Kubernetes cluster architecture.

The fundamental goal of Kubernetes is to help you manage your containers. The Pod is the minimal piece deployable in a Kubernetes cluster, containing one or several containers.

From the kubectl command line, you can run a Pod containing a container as simply as running this command:

```
$ kubectl run nginx --image=nginx
pod/nginx created
```

By adding --dry-run=client -o yaml to the command, you can see the YAML template you would have to write to create the same Pod:

```
$ kubectl run nginx --image=nginx --dry-run=client -o yaml
apiVersion: v1
kind: Pod
metadata:
  creationTimestamp: null
  labels:
    run: nginx
  name: nginx
spec:
  containers:
  - image: nginx
    name: nginx
    resources: {}
```

© Philippe Martin 2021
P. Martin, *Kubernetes*, https://doi.org/10.1007/978-1-4842-6494-2_5

```
  dnsPolicy: ClusterFirst
  restartPolicy: Always
status: {}
```

Or you can greatly simplify the template by keeping only the required fields:

```
-- simple.yaml
apiVersion: v1
kind: Pod
metadata:
  name: nginx
spec:
  containers:
  - name: nginx
    image: nginx
```

You can now start the Pod by using this template:

```
$ kubectl apply -f simple.yaml
pod/nginx created
```

The Pod created is ready...if you are not very fussy. Otherwise, the Pod offers a long list of fields to make it more production-ready. Here are all these fields.

Pod Specs

Here is a classification of the Pod specification fields:

- **Containers** fields will define and parameterize more precisely each container of the Pod, whether it is a normal container (containers) or an init container (initContainers). The imagePullSecrets field will help to download container images from private registries.

- **Volumes** field (volumes) will define a list of volumes that containers will be able to mount and share.

- **Scheduling** fields will help you define the most appropriate node to deploy the Pod, by selecting nodes by labels (nodeSelector), directly specifying a node name (nodeName), using affinity and tolerations, by selecting a specific scheduler (schedulerName), and by requiring a specific runtime class (runtimeClassName). They will also be used to prioritize a Pod over other Pods (priorityClassName and priority).

- **Lifecycle** fields will help define if a Pod should restart after termination (restartPolicy) and fine-tune the periods after which processes running in the containers of a terminating Pod are killed (terminationGracePeriodSeconds) or after which a running Pod will be stopped if not yet terminated (activeDeadlineSeconds). They also help define readiness of a Pod (readinessGates).

- **Hostname and Name resolution** fields will help define the hostname (hostname) and part of the FQDN (subdomain) of the Pod, add hosts in the */etc/hosts* files of the containers (hostAliases), fine-tune the */etc/resolv.conf* files of the containers (dnsConfig), and define a policy for the DNS configuration (dnsPolicy).

- **Host namespaces** fields will help indicate if the Pod must use host namespaces for network (hostNetwork), PIDs (hostPID), and IPC (hostIPC) and if containers will share the same (non-host) process namespace (shareProcessNamespace).

- **Service account** fields will be useful to give specific rights to a Pod, by affecting it a specific service account (serviceAccountName) or by disabling the automount of the default service account with automountService AccountToken.

- **Security context** field (securityContext) helps define various security attributes and common container settings at the Pod level.

Container Specs

An important part of the definition of a Pod is the definition of the containers it will contain.

We can separate containers fields into two parts. The first part contains fields that are related to the container runtime (image, entrypoint, ports, environment variables, and volumes); the second part contains fields that will be handled by the Kubernetes system.

The fields related to container runtime are as follows:

- **Image** fields define the image of the container (image) and the policy to pull the image (imagePullPolicy).

- **Entrypoint** fields define the command (command) and arguments (args) of the entrypoint and its working directory (workingDir).

- **Ports** field (ports) defines the list of ports to expose from the container.

- **Environment variables** fields help define the environment variables that will be exported in the container, either directly (env) or by referencing ConfigMap or Secret values (envFrom).

- **Volumes** fields define the volumes to mount into the container, whether they are a filesystem volume (`volumeMounts`) or a raw block volume (`volumeDevices`).

The fields related to Kubernetes are as follows:

- **Resources** field (`resources`) helps define the resource requirements and limits for a container.

- **Lifecycle** fields help define handlers on lifecycle events (`lifecycle`), parameterize the termination message (`terminationMessagePath` and `terminationMessagePolicy`), and define probes to check liveness (`livenessProbe`) and readiness (`readinessProbe`) of the container.

- **Security context** field helps define various security attributes and common container settings at the container level.

- **Debugging** fields are very specialized fields, mostly for debugging purposes (`stdin`, `stdinOnce`, and `tty`).

Pod Controllers

The Pod, although being the masterpiece of the Kubernetes architecture, is rarely used alone. You will generally use a controller to run a Pod with some specific policies.

The different controllers handling Pods are as follows:

- `ReplicaSet`: Ensures that a specified number of Pod replicas are running at any given time.

- `Deployment`: Enables declarative updates for Pods and ReplicaSets.

- StatefulSet: Manages updates of Pods and ReplicaSets, taking care of stateful resources.

- DaemonSet: Ensures that all or some nodes are running a copy of a Pod.

- Job: Starts Pods and ensures they complete.

- CronJob: Creates a Job on a time-based schedule.

In Kubernetes, all controllers respect the principle of the **Reconcile Loop**: the controller perpetually **watches** for some objects of interest, to be able to detect if the actual state of the cluster (the objects running into the cluster) satisfies the specs of the different objects the controller is responsible for and to adapt the cluster consequently.

Let's take a closer look at how ReplicaSet and Deployment controllers work.

ReplicaSet Controller

Fields for a ReplicaSet are as follows:

- replicas indicates how many replicas of selected Pods you want.

- selector defines the Pods you want the ReplicaSet controller to manage.

- template is the template used to create new Pods when insufficient replicas are detected by the controller.

- minReadySeconds indicates the number of seconds the controller should wait after a Pod starts without failing to consider the Pod is ready.

The ReplicaSet controller perpetually **watches** the Pods with the labels specified with `selector`. At any given time, if the number of actual running Pods with these labels

- Is greater than the requested `replicas`, some Pods will be terminated to satisfy the number of replicas. Note that the terminated Pods are not necessarily Pods that were created by the ReplicaSet controller.

- Is lower than the requested `replicas`, new Pods will be created with the specified Pod `template` to satisfy the number of replicas. Note that to avoid the ReplicaSet controller to create Pods in a loop, the specified `template` must create a Pod selectable by the specified `selector` (this is the reason why you must set the same labels in the `selector.matchLabels` and `template.metadata.labels` fields).

Note that

- The `selector` field of a ReplicaSet is immutable.

- Changing the `template` of a ReplicaSet will not have an immediate effect. It will affect the Pods that will be created after this change.

- Changing the `replicas` field will immediately trigger the creation or termination of Pods.

Deployment Controller

Fields for a Deployment are as follows:

- `replicas` indicates the number of replicas requested.

- `selector` defines the Pods you want the Deployment controller to manage.

29

- `template` is the template requested for the Pods.

- `minReadySeconds` indicates the number of seconds the controller should wait after a Pod starts without failing to consider the Pod is ready.

- `strategy` is the strategy to apply when changing the `replicas` of the previously and currently active `ReplicaSets`.

- `revisionHistoryLimit` is the number of `ReplicaSets` to keep for future use.

- `paused` indicates if the Deployment is active or not.

- `progressDeadlineSeconds`.

The Deployment controller perpetually **watches** the ReplicaSets with the requested `selector`. Among these

- If a ReplicaSet with the requested `template` exists, the controller will ensure that the number of replicas for this ReplicaSet equals the number of requested `replicas` (by using the requested `strategy`), and `minReadySeconds` equals the requested one.

- If no ReplicaSet exists with the requested `template`, the controller will create a new ReplicaSet with the requested `replicas`, `selector`, `template`, and `minReadySeconds`.

- For ReplicaSets with a non-matching `template`, the controller will ensure that the number of `replicas` is set to zero (by using the requested `strategy`).

Note that

- The `selector` field of a Deployment is immutable.

- Changing the `template` field of a Deployment will immediately

  - Either trigger the creation of a new ReplicaSet if no one exists with the requested `selector` and `template`

  - Or update an existing one matching the requested `selector` and `template` with the requested `replicas` (using `strategy`)

  - Or set to zero the number of `replicas` of other ReplicaSets

- Changing the `replicas` or `minReadySeconds` field of a Deployment will immediately update the corresponding value of the corresponding ReplicaSet (the one with the requested `template`).

With this method, the Deployment controller manages a series of ReplicaSets, one for each revision of the Pod template. The active ReplicaSet is the one with a positive number of replicas, the other revisions having a number of replicas set to zero.

This way, you can switch from one revision to another (e.g., for a rollback) by switching the Pod template from one revision to another.

Update and Rollback

Let's first deploy an image of the nginx server, with the help of a Deployment:

```
$ kubectl create deployment nginx --image=nginx:1.10
deployment.apps/nginx created
```

The command kubectl rollout provides several subcommands to work with Deployments.

The subcommand status gives us the status of the Deployment:

```
$ kubectl rollout status deployment nginx
deployment "nginx" successfully rolled out
```

The history subcommand gives us the history of revisions for the Deployment. Here the Deployment is at its first revision:

```
$ kubectl rollout history deployment nginx
deployment.apps/nginx
REVISION   CHANGE-CAUSE
1          <none>
```

We will now update the image of nginx to use the 1.11 revision. One way is to use the kubectl set image command:

```
$ kubectl set image deployment nginx nginx=nginx:1.11
deployment.extensions/nginx image updated
```

We can see with the history subcommand that the Deployment is at its second revision:

```
$ kubectl rollout history deployment nginx
deployment.apps/nginx
REVISION   CHANGE-CAUSE
1          <none>
2          <none>
```

The change-cause is empty by default. It can contain the command used to make the rollout either by using the --record flag

```
$ kubectl set image deployment nginx nginx=nginx:1.12 --record
deployment.apps/nginx image updated
$ kubectl rollout history deployment nginx
```

```
deployment.apps/nginx
REVISION   CHANGE-CAUSE
1          <none>
2          <none>
3          kubectl set image deployment nginx
           nginx=nginx:1.12 --record=true
```

or by setting the kubernetes.io/change-cause annotation after the rollout:

```
$ kubectl set image deployment nginx nginx=nginx:1.13
deployment.apps/nginx image updated
$ kubectl annotate deployment nginx \
  kubernetes.io/change-cause="update to revision 1.13" \
  --record=false --overwrite=true
$ kubectl rollout history deployment nginx
deployment.apps/nginx
REVISION   CHANGE-CAUSE
1          <none>
2          <none>
3          kubectl set image deployment nginx
           nginx=nginx:1.12 --record=true
4          update to revision 1.13
```

It is also possible to edit the specifications of the Deployment:

```
$ kubectl edit deployment nginx
```

After your preferred editor opens, you can, for example, add an environment variable FOO=bar to the specification of the container:

```
[...]
    spec:
      containers:
      - image: nginx:1.13
```

```
        env:
      - name: FOO
        value: bar
[...]
```

After you save the template and quit the editor, the new revision is deployed. Let's verify that the new Pod contains this environment variable:

```
$ kubectl describe pod -l app=nginx
[...]
    Environment:
      FOO:  bar
[...]
```

Let's set a change-cause for this release and see the history:

```
$ kubectl annotate deployment nginx \
  kubernetes.io/change-cause="add FOO environment variable" \
  --record=false --overwrite=true
$ kubectl rollout history deployment nginx
deployment.apps/nginx
REVISION   CHANGE-CAUSE
1          <none>
2          <none>
3          kubectl set image deployment nginx
           nginx=nginx:1.12 --record=true
4          update to revision 1.13
5          add FOO environment variable
```

Now let's roll back the last rollout with the undo subcommand:

```
$ kubectl rollout undo deployment nginx
deployment.apps/nginx rolled back
$ kubectl rollout history deployment nginx
deployment.apps/nginx
```

```
REVISION   CHANGE-CAUSE
1          <none>
2          <none>
3          kubectl set image deployment nginx
           nginx=nginx:1.12 --record=true
5          add FOO envvar
6          update to revision 1.13
```

We see that we switched back to the fourth release (which disappeared in the list and has been renamed as the sixth revision).

It is also possible to roll back to a specific revision, for example, to use the nginx:1.12 image again:

```
$ kubectl rollout undo deployment nginx --to-revision=3
deployment.apps/nginx rolled back
$ kubectl rollout history deployment nginx
deployment.apps/nginx
REVISION   CHANGE-CAUSE
1          <none>
2          <none>
5          add FOO envvar
6          update to revision 1.13
7          kubectl set image deployment nginx
           nginx=nginx:1.12 --record=true
```

Finally, you can verify that one ReplicaSet exists for each revision:

```
$ kubectl get replicaset
NAME               DESIRED CURRENT READY AGE
nginx-65c8969d67   0       0       0     58m
nginx-68b47b4d58   0       0       0     62m
nginx-7856959c59   1       1       1     62m
nginx-84c7fd7848   0       0       0     62m
nginx-857df58577   0       0       0     62m
```

Deployment Strategies

You have seen in the "Deployment Controller" section that the Deployment controller provides different **strategies** when changing the number of replicas of the old and new ReplicaSets.

The Recreate Strategy

The simplest strategy is the **Recreate** strategy: in this case, the old ReplicaSet will be downsized to zero, and when all Pods of this ReplicaSet are stopped, the new ReplicaSet will be upsized to the number of requested replicas.

Some consequences are as follows:

- There will be a small downtime, the time the old Pods stop and the new Pods start.

- No additional resources are necessary to run previous and new Pods in parallel.

- Old and new versions will not run simultaneously.

The RollingUpdate Strategy

The **RollingUpdate** strategy is a more advanced strategy, and the one by default when you create a Deployment.

The goal of this strategy is to update from previous to new version without downtime.

This strategy will combine the possibility to downsize and upsize ReplicaSets and the possibility to expose Pods through Services.

You will see in Chapter 10 that Pods are traditionally accessed through Services. A Service resource declares a list of endpoints, which are the list of Pods that are exposed through this Service. Pods are removed from endpoints of Services when they are **not ready** to serve requests and are added when they become **ready** to serve requests.

The readiness of a Pod is determined by the state of the **readiness probes** declared for its containers. If you do not declare readiness probes for your containers, the risk is that the Pods are detected ready before they really are and traffic is sent to them while they are still in their startup phase.

During a rolling update, the Deployment controller will on the one hand

- Upsize the number of replicas of the new versions
- When a replica is ready, it will be added to the Service endpoints by the Endpoints controller.

and on the other hand

- Mark replicas of old versions not ready, so they are removed from the Service endpoints by the Endpoints controller
- Stop these replicas

Depending on traffic and available resources, you may want to either first augment the number of new versions of replicas and then stop old replicas or conversely first stop old replicas and then start new versions of replicas.

For this, the fields `maxSurge` and `maxUnavailable` of the Deployment `strategy` field indicate how many replicas can be present, respectively, in addition to and less than the expected number of replicas. Depending on these values, the Deployment controller will either first start new versions or conversely first stop old versions.

Running Jobs

Job and CronJob controllers help you run Pods until they complete and on a time-based schedule.

Job Controller

The Job controller runs one or more Pods in parallel and waits for a specific number of these Pods to terminate successfully.

Run One Pod to Its Completion

The simplest case is to run one Pod to its completion. In this case, you have to declare the template of the Pod you want to run with `spec.template`, and the Job controller will start a Pod from this template.

If, after a while, the Pod terminates with success (this means that all containers exit with a Zero status), the job is marked as completed.

But if the Pod exits in error, a new Pod will be restarted until the Pod succeeds or until a given number of errors occur. The number of retries is determined by the value of `spec.backoffLimit`.

Here is an example of a job that will run to its completion:

```
apiVersion: batch/v1
kind: Job
metadata:
  name: a-job
spec:
  template:
    spec:
      containers:
      - name: a-job
```

```
    image: bash
    command: ["bash", "-c", "sleep 1; exit 0" ]
  restartPolicy: Never
```

After a few seconds, you would see that the Pod status is Completed and the job status is succeeded:

```
$ kubectl get pods
NAME            READY    STATUS       RESTARTS    AGE
a-job-sgd8r     0/1      Completed    0           8s

$ kubectl get jobs
NAME      COMPLETIONS    DURATION    AGE
a-job     1/1            4s          60s

$ kubectl get jobs a-job -o yaml
[...]
status:
  completionTime: "2020-08-15T09:19:07Z"
  conditions:
  - lastProbeTime: "2020-08-15T09:19:07Z"
    lastTransitionTime: "2020-08-15T09:19:07Z"
    status: "True"
    type: Complete
  startTime: "2020-08-15T09:19:03Z"
  succeeded: 1
```

Now, here is an example of a job that will constantly fail:

```
apiVersion: batch/v1
kind: Job
metadata:
  name: a-job-failing
```

```
spec:
  template:
    spec:
      containers:
      - name: a-job-failing
        image: bash
        command: ["bash", "-c", "sleep 1; exit 1" ]
      restartPolicy: Never
  backoffLimit: 3
```

After a while, you can see that four Pods (one plus three retries) have been started and all these Pods have failed and the job is marked as failed:

```
$ kubectl get pods
NAME                     READY   STATUS   RESTARTS   AGE
a-job-failing-92qsj      0/1     Error    0          2m19s
a-job-failing-c5w9x      0/1     Error    0          2m5s
a-job-failing-g4bp9      0/1     Error    0          105s
a-job-failing-nwm4q      0/1     Error    0          2m15s

$ kubectl get jobs a-job-failing -o yaml
[...]
status:
  conditions:
  - lastProbeTime: "2020-08-15T09:26:14Z"
    lastTransitionTime: "2020-08-15T09:26:14Z"
    message: Job has reached the specified backoff limit
    reason: BackoffLimitExceeded
    status: "True"
    type: Failed
  failed: 4
  startTime: "2020-08-15T09:25:00Z"
```

Run Several Pods Until One Completes

If you specify a number of Pods to run in parallel with `spec.parallelism` and do not define a number of completions in `spec.completions`, the Job controller will run this number of Pods in parallel until one succeeds.

During the time before the first Pod succeeds, the failed Pods will be replaced by other Pods. Once one Pod succeeds, the controller will wait for other Pods to terminate (in error or success) and will mark the Job as succeeded.

With this example running four Pods in parallel, exiting randomly in error or in success, you can examine how the controller acts:

```
apiVersion: batch/v1
kind: Job
metadata:
  name: a-job
spec:
  template:
    spec:
      containers:
      - name: a-job
        image: bash
        command: ["bash", "-c", "sleep $((RANDOM/1024+1)); exit
        $((RANDOM/16384))" ]
  restartPolicy: Never
parallelism: 4
```

```
$ kubectl apply -f job-parallel.yaml && kubectl get pods -w
job.batch/a-job created
NAME            READY   STATUS              RESTARTS  AGE
a-job-aaaaa     0/1     ContainerCreating   0         2s
a-job-bbbbb     0/1     ContainerCreating   0         2s
a-job-ccccc     0/1     ContainerCreating   0         2s
```

41

```
a-job-ddddd  0/1   ContainerCreating  0    3s
a-job-aaaaa  1/1   Running            0    5s
a-job-bbbbb  1/1   Running            0    6s
a-job-ccccc  1/1   Running            0    7s
a-job-ddddd  1/1   Running            0    8s
a-job-bbbbb  0/1   Error              0    12s b fails
a-job-BBBBB  0/1   Pending            0    0s B replaces b
a-job-BBBBB  0/1   ContainerCreating  0    0s
a-job-BBBBB  1/1   Running            0    3s
a-job-aaaaa  0/1   Error              0    19s a fails
a-job-AAAAA  0/1   Pending            0    0s A replaces a
a-job-AAAAA  0/1   ContainerCreating  0    0s
a-job-ddddd  0/1   Completed          0    22s d succeeds
a-job-AAAAA  1/1   Running            0    3s
a-job-AAAAA  0/1   Error              0    6s A fails, not
                                            replaced
a-job-ccccc  0/1   Error              0    29s c fails,
                                            not replaced
a-job-BBBBB  0/1   Completed          0    36s B succeeds
```

Run Several Pods Until Several Pods Complete

You can specify with spec.completions how many Pods you want to succeed and with spec.parallelism the maximum number of Pods to run in parallel.

In all cases, the number of Pods running in parallel will never be higher than the number of completions still to be done. For example, if you specify a completions of 4 and a parallelism of 6, the controller will first start four Pods (because there are still four completions to be done). When a first Pod succeeds, there are three completions left, and the controller will not start a new Pod if there are already three Pods running.

In this example, let's examine how the controller acts for a parallelism of 4 and a completions of 4:

```
apiVersion: batch/v1
kind: Job
metadata:
  name: a-job
spec:
  template: spec:
    containers:
    - name: a-job
      image: bash
      command: ["bash", "-c", "sleep $((RANDOM/1024+1)); exit
      $((RANDOM/16384))" ]
    restartPolicy: Never
  parallelism: 4
  completions: 4
```

```
$ kubectl apply -f job-parallel.yaml && kubectl get pods -w
job.batch/a-job created
NAME            READY   STATUS              RESTARTS   AGE
a-job-aaa01     0/1     ContainerCreating   0          1s
a-job-bbb01     0/1     ContainerCreating   0          1s
a-job-ccc01     0/1     ContainerCreating   0          1s
a-job-ddd01     0/1     ContainerCreating   0          1s
a-job-ccc01     1/1     Running             0          5s
a-job-bbb01     1/1     Running             0          5s
```

a-job-aaa01	1/1	Running	0	7s
a-job-ddd01	1/1	Running	0	9s
a-job-ccc01	0/1	Completed	0	11s c1 succeeds
a-job-ddd01	0/1	Completed	0	13s d1 succeeds
a-job-aaa01	0/1	Completed	0	17s a1 succeeds
a-job-bbb01	0/1	Error	0	28s b1 fails, replaced by b2
a-job-bbb02	0/1	Pending	0	0s
a-job-bbb02	0/1	ContainerCreating	0	0s
a-job-bbb02	1/1	Running	0	4s
a-job-bbb02	0/1	Error	0	30s b2 fails, replaced by b3
a-job-bbb03	0/1	Pending	0	0s
a-job-bbb03	0/1	ContainerCreating	0	0s
a-job-bbb03	1/1	Running	0	3s
a-job-bbb03	0/1	Completed	0	12s b3 succeeds

CronJob Controller

The CronJob controller permits you to run Jobs on a time-based schedule.

When creating a CronJob template, the two required spec fields are the following:

- jobTemplate is the template of the Job you want to run on a time-based schedule.

- schedule is the time specification at which to run the Job, in Cron format.

The concurrencyPolicy indicates how to treat a new Job when a previous job is still running. The possible values are Allow to allow several concurrent Jobs, Forbid to skip the new Job if the previous one is still running, and Replace to first cancel the previous Job before running the new one.

The suspend Boolean value is useful if you want to temporarily suspend a specific CronJob, without deleting it.

Schedule Format

The schedule information is made of five parts, representing the time to execute the job:

- Minute (0–59)

- Hour (0–23)

- Day of the month (1–31)

- Month (1–12)

- Day of the week (0 – Sunday to 6 – Saturday)

You can use a star * if you do not want to restrict on a specific field.

The notation */n where n is a number can be used to run the Job every nth interval of time.

You can separate values with commas to specify several time intervals.

Examples:

- 10 2 * * * will run the job every day at 2:10 AM.

- 30 3 * * 0 will run the job every Sunday at 3:30 AM.

- */15 7,8,9 * * * will run the job every 15 minutes between 7 AM and 10 AM (excluded).

CHAPTER 6

Configuring Applications

An application can be configured in different ways:

- By passing arguments to the command
- By defining environment variables
- Using configuration files

Arguments to the Command

We have seen in Chapter 5, section "Container Specs," that we can define the arguments of the command with the Args field of the Container spec.

It is not possible to define the arguments of the command imperatively by using the kubectl command run or create.

Depending on the definition of the image, it is possible you have to also specify the Command value (especially if the Dockerfile does not define an ENTRYPOINT but only a CMD).

© Philippe Martin 2021
P. Martin, *Kubernetes*, https://doi.org/10.1007/978-1-4842-6494-2_6

You have to specify the arguments in the template defining the container:

```
apiVersion: apps/v1
kind: Deployment
metadata:
  name: nginx
  labels:
    app: nginx
spec:
  replicas: 1
  selector:
    matchLabels:
      app: nginx
  template:
    metadata:
      labels:
        app: nginx
    spec:
      containers:
      - image: nginx
        name: nginx
        command: ["nginx"]
        args: ["-g", "daemon off; worker_priority 10;"]
```

Environment Variables

It is possible to define environment variables for a container either by declaring their values directly or by referencing their values from ConfigMaps, Secrets, or fields of the object created (Deployment and others).

Declaring Values Directly

In Declarative Form

Declaratively, you can add environment variables to the definition of a
container:

```
apiVersion: apps/v1
kind: Deployment
metadata:
  labels:
    app: nginx
  name: nginx
spec:
  replicas: 1
  selector:
    matchLabels:
      app: nginx
  template:
    metadata:
      labels:
        app: nginx
    spec:
      containers:
      - image: nginx
        name: nginx
        env:
        - name: VAR1
          value: "value1"
        - name: VAR2
          value: "value2"
```

In Imperative Form

Imperatively, using the kubectl run command, you can define
environment variables from the command line:

```
$ kubectl run nginx --image=nginx \
  --env VAR1=value1 \
  --env VAR2=value2
pod/nginx created
```

Note that the variant of the kubectl run command to create a
Deployment is deprecated, in favor of the kubectl create deployment
command. Unfortunately, the --env flag is not accepted by this command.
You can instead use the kubectl set env command to add environment
variables after you create the Deployment:

```
$ kubectl create deployment nginx --image=nginx
deployment.apps/nginx created
$ kubectl set env deployment nginx \
  --env VAR1=value1 \
  --env VAR2=value2
deployment.apps/nginx env updated
```

Referencing Specific Values from ConfigMaps and Secrets

In Declarative Form

Declaratively, when declaring an environment variable, you can indicate
that the values should be extracted from a ConfigMap or Secret, one by
one:

```
apiVersion: v1
kind: ConfigMap
metadata:
  name: vars
data:
  var1: value1
  var2: value2
---
apiVersion: v1
kind: Secret
metadata:
  name: passwords
stringData:
  pass1: foo
---
apiVersion: apps/v1
kind: Deployment
metadata:
  labels:
    app: nginx
  name: nginx
spec:
  replicas: 1
  selector:
    matchLabels:
      app: nginx
  template:
    metadata:
      labels:
        app: nginx
```

```
spec:
  containers:
  - image: nginx
    name: nginx
    env:
    - name: VAR1
      valueFrom:
        configMapKeyRef:
            key: var1
            name: vars
    - name: VAR2
      valueFrom:
        configMapKeyRef:
            key: var2
            name: vars
    - name: PASS1
      valueFrom:
        secretKeyRef:
            key: pass1
            name: passwords
```

Note that if the referenced key is not found in the referenced
ConfigMaps or Secrets, the creation of the Deployment will fail. If you want
to create the Deployment even if a value does not exist (in this case, the
corresponding environment variable will not be defined), you can use the
optional field:

```
- name: PASS2
  valueFrom:
    secretKeyRef:
        key: pass2
        name: passwords
        optional: true
```

In Imperative Form

Imperatively, you can also use the kubectl set env command with
the --from and keys flags. In this example, you reference only some of the
keys defined in the ConfigMap and Secret:

```
$ kubectl create configmap vars \
  --from-literal=var1=value1 \
  --from-literal=var2=value2 \
  --from-literal=var3=value3
configmap/vars created
$ kubectl create secret generic passwords \
  --from-literal=pass1=foo \
  --from-literal=pass2=bar
secret/passwords created
$ kubectl create deployment nginx --image=nginx
deployment.apps/nginx created
$ kubectl set env deployment nginx \
  --from=configmap/vars \
  --keys="var1,var2"
deployment.apps/nginx env updated
$ kubectl set env deployment nginx \
  --from=secret/passwords \
  --keys="pass1"
deployment.apps/nginx env updated
```

Referencing All Values from ConfigMaps and Secrets

In Declarative Form

You can also inject all the entries of a ConfigMap or Secret as environment variables (you can also use in this case the `optional` field to indicate that the operation should succeed even if the referenced ConfigMap or Secret does not exist):

```
apiVersion: v1
kind: ConfigMap
metadata:
  name: vars
data:
  var1: value1
  var2: value2
---
apiVersion: v1
kind: Secret
metadata:
  name: passwords
stringData:
  pass1: foo
---
apiVersion: apps/v1
kind: Deployment
metadata:
  labels:
    app: nginx
  name: nginx
```

```
spec:
  replicas: 1
  selector:
    matchLabels:
      app:  nginx
  template:
    metadata:
      labels:
        app: nginx
    spec:
      containers:
      - image: nginx
        name: nginx
        envFrom:
        - configMapRef:
            name: vars
        - secretRef:
            name: passwords
        - secretRef:
            name: notfound
            optional: true
```

In Imperative Form

Imperatively, you can also use the kubectl set env command with
the --from flags:

```
$ kubectl create configmap vars \
  --from-literal=var1=value1 \
  --from-literal=var2=value2
configmap/vars created
```

```
$ kubectl create secret generic passwords \
  --from-literal=pass1=foo
secret/passwords created
$ kubectl create deployment nginx --image=nginx
deployment.apps/nginx created
$ kubectl set env deployment nginx \
  --from=configmap/vars
deployment.apps/nginx env updated
$ kubectl set env deployment nginx \
  --from=secret/passwords
deployment.apps/nginx env updated
```

Referencing Values from Pod Fields

Declaratively, it is possible to reference the value of some fields of the Pod:

- metadata.name

- metadata.namespace

- metadata.uid

- spec.nodeName

- spec.serviceAccountName

- status.hostIP

- status.podIP

```
apiVersion: apps/v1
kind: Deployment
metadata:
  labels:
    app: nginx
  name: nginx
```

```
spec:
  replicas: 1
  selector:
    matchLabels:
      app: nginx
  template:
    metadata:
      labels:
        app: nginx
    spec:
      containers:
      - image: nginx
        name: nginx
        env:
        - name: POD_NAME
          valueFrom:
            fieldRef:
                fieldPath: metadata.name
        - name: POD_NAMESPACE
          valueFrom:
            fieldRef:
                fieldPath: metadata.namespace
        - name: POD_UID
          valueFrom:
            fieldRef:
                fieldPath: metadata.uid
        - name:    POD_NODENAME
          valueFrom:
            fieldRef:
                fieldPath: spec.nodeName
        - name: POD_SERVICEACCOUNTNAME
```

57

```
      valueFrom:
        fieldRef:
            fieldPath: spec.serviceAccountName
  - name: POD_HOSTIP
      valueFrom:
        fieldRef:
            fieldPath: status.hostIP
  - name: POD_PODIP
      valueFrom:
        fieldRef:
            fieldPath: status.podIP
```

After applying this template, you can examine the values of the environment variables into the container:

```
$ kubectl exec -it nginx-xxxxxxxxxx-yyyyy bash -- -c "env |
grep POD_"
```

Referencing Values from Container Resources Fields

Declaratively, it is possible to reference the values of resource requests and limits for a container. You can use the divisor field to divide the value by the given divisor:

```
apiVersion: apps/v1
kind: Deployment
metadata:
  labels:
    app: nginx
  name: nginx
```

```
spec:
  replicas: 1
  selector:
    matchLabels:
      app: nginx
  template:
    metadata:
      labels:
        app: nginx
    spec:
      containers:
      - image: nginx
        name: nginx
        resources:
          requests:
            cpu: "500m"
            memory: "500Mi"
          limits:
            cpu: "1"
            memory: "1Gi"
        env:
        - name: M_CPU_REQUEST
          valueFrom:
            resourceFieldRef:
                resource: requests.cpu
                divisor: "0.001"
        - name: MEMORY_REQUEST
          valueFrom:
            resourceFieldRef:
                resource: requests.memory
        - name:  M_CPU_LIMIT
```

```
        valueFrom:
          resourceFieldRef:
              resource: limits.cpu
              divisor: "0.001"
      - name: MEMORY_LIMIT
        valueFrom:
          resourceFieldRef:
              resource: limits.memory
```

The variables will get the following values:

```
M_CPU_REQUEST=500
MEMORY_REQUEST=524288000
M_CPU_LIMIT=1000
MEMORY_LIMIT=1073741824
```

Configuration File from ConfigMap

It is possible to mount ConfigMap contents in the container filesystem. Each key/value of the mounted ConfigMap will be a filename and its content in the mount directory.

For example, you can create this ConfigMap in declarative form:

```
apiVersion: v1
kind: ConfigMap
metadata:
  name: config
data:
  nginx.conf: |
    server {
      location / {
        root /data/www;
      }
```

```
    location /images/ {
      root /data;
    }
  }
```

or in imperative form:

```
$ cat > nginx.conf <<EOF
server {
    location / {
        root /data/www;
    }

    location /images/ {
        root /data;
    }
}
EOF
$ kubectl create configmap config --from-file=nginx.conf
configmap/config created
```

Then you can mount the ConfigMap in the container:

```
apiVersion: apps/v1
kind: Deployment
metadata:
  labels:
    app: nginx
  name: nginx
spec:
  replicas:  1
  selector:
    matchLabels:
      app: nginx
    template:
```

```
metadata:
  labels:
    app: nginx
spec:
  volumes:
  - name: config-volume
    configMap: config
  containers:
  - image: nginx
    name: nginx
    volumeMounts:
    - name: config-volume
      mountPath: /etc/nginx/conf.d/
```

Finally, the file /etc/nginx/conf.d/nginx.conf in the container will contain the value of the nginx.conf key of the ConfigMap.

Configuration File from Secret

Similarly, it is possible to mount the contents of Secrets. First, create a Secret, in declarative form

```
apiVersion: v1
kind: Secret
metadata:
  name: passwords
stringData:
  password: foobar
```

or imperative form:

```
$ kubectl create secret generic passwords \
  --from-literal=password=foobar
secret/passwords created
```

Then mount the Secret in the container:

```
apiVersion: apps/v1
kind: Deployment
metadata:
  labels:
    app: nginx
  name: nginx
spec:
  replicas: 1
  selector:
    matchLabels:
      app: nginx
  template:
    metadata:
      labels:
        app: nginx
    spec:
      volumes:
      - name: passwords-volume
        secret:
          secretName: passwords
          containers:
          - image: nginx
            name: nginx
            volumeMounts:
            - name: passwords-volume
              mountPath: /etc/passwords
```

Finally, the file /etc/passwords/password in the container will contain foobar.

Configuration File from Pod Fields

Declaratively, it is possible to mount a volume with files containing Pod values:

- metadata.name

- metadata.namespace

- metadata.uid

- metadata.labels

- metadata.annotations

```
apiVersion: apps/v1
kind: Deployment
metadata:
  labels:
    app: nginx
  name: nginx
spec:
  replicas: 1
  selector:
    matchLabels:
      app: nginx
  template:
    metadata:
      labels:
        app: nginx
    spec:
      containers:
      - image: nginx
        name: nginx
        volumeMounts:
```

```
    - name: pod-info
      mountPath: /pod
      readOnly: true
  volumes:
    - name: pod-info
      downwardAPI:
        items:
        - path: metadata/name
          fieldRef:
            fieldPath: metadata.name
        - path: metadata/namespace
          fieldRef:
            fieldPath: metadata.namespace
        - path: metadata/uid
          fieldRef:
            fieldPath: metadata.uid
        - path: metadata/labels
          fieldRef:
            fieldPath: metadata.labels
        - path: metadata/annotations
          fieldRef:
            fieldPath: metadata.annotations
```

As a result, in the container, you can find files in /pod/metadata:

```
$ kubectl exec nginx-xxxxxxxxxx-yyyyy bash -- -c \
  'for i in /pod/metadata/*; do echo $i; cat -n $i; echo ; done'
/pod/metadata/annotations
    1  kubernetes.io/config.seen="2020-01-
       11T17:21:40.497901295Z"
    2  kubernetes.io/config.source="api"
       /pod/metadata/labels
```

```
  1   app="nginx"
  2   pod-template-hash="789ccf5b7b"
      /pod/metadata/name
  1   nginx-xxxxxxxxxx-yyyyy
      /pod/metadata/namespace
  1   default
      /pod/metadata/uid
  1   631d01b2-eb1c-49dc-8c06-06d244f74ed4
```

Configuration File from Container Resources Fields

Declaratively, it is possible to mount a volume with files containing the values of resource requests and limits for a container. You can use the divisor field to divide the value by the given divisor:

```
apiVersion: apps/v1
kind: Deployment
metadata:
  labels:
    app: nginx
  name: nginx
spec:
  replicas: 1
  selector:
    matchLabels:
      app: nginx
  template:
    metadata:
      labels:
        app: nginx
    spec:
```

```
containers:
- image: nginx
  name: nginx
  resources:
    requests:
      cpu: "500m"
      memory: "500Mi"
    limits:
      cpu: "1"
      memory: "1Gi"
  volumeMounts:
  - name: resources-info
    mountPath: /resources
    readOnly: true
volumes:
  - name: resources-info
    downwardAPI:
      items:
      - path: limits/cpu
        resourceFieldRef:
          resource: limits.cpu
          divisor: "0.001"
          containerName: nginx
      - path: limits/memory
        resourceFieldRef:
          resource: limits.memory
          containerName: nginx
      - path: requests/cpu
        resourceFieldRef:
          resource: requests.cpu
          divisor: "0.001"
          containerName: nginx
```

```
    - path: requests/memory
      resourceFieldRef:
        resource: requests.memory
        containerName: nginx
```

As a result, in the container, you can find files in /resources:

```
$ kubectl exec nginx-85d7c97f64-9knh9 bash -- -c \
  'for i in /resources/*/*; do echo $i; cat -n $i; echo ; done'
/resources/limits/cpu
    1   1000
/resources/limits/memory
    1   1073741824
/resources/requests/cpu
    1   500
/resources/requests/memory
    1   524288000
```

Configuration File from Different Sources

It is possible to mount volumes with files containing information from a mix of ConfigMaps, Secrets, Pod fields, and container resources fields.

The main difference with previous examples is that it is here possible to mix values from these different sources inside the same directory:

```
apiVersion: v1
kind: ConfigMap
metadata:
  name: values
data:
  cpu: "4000"
  memory: "17179869184"
---
```

```yaml
apiVersion: apps/v1
kind: Deployment
metadata:
  labels:
    app: nginx
  name: nginx
spec:
  replicas: 1
  selector:
    matchLabels:
      app: nginx
  template:
    metadata:
      labels:
        app: nginx
    spec:
      containers:
      - image: nginx
        name: nginx
        resources:
          requests:
            cpu: "500m"
            memory: "500Mi"
          limits:
            cpu: "1"
            memory: "1Gi"
        volumeMounts:
        - name: config
          mountPath: /config
          readOnly: true
```

```
volumes:
  - name: config
    projected:
      sources:
      - configMap:
          name: values
          items:
          - key: cpu
            path: cpu/value
          - key: memory
            path: memory/value
      - downwardAPI:
          items:
          - path: cpu/limits
            resourceFieldRef:
              resource: limits.cpu
              divisor: "0.001"
              containerName: nginx
          - path: memory/limits
            resourceFieldRef:
              resource: limits.memory
              containerName: nginx
          - path: cpu/requests
            resourceFieldRef:
              resource: requests.cpu
              divisor: "0.001"
              containerName: nginx
          - path: memory/requests
            resourceFieldRef:
              resource: requests.memory
              containerName: nginx
```

As a result, in the container, you can find files in /config:

```
$ kubectl exec nginx-7d797b5788-xzw79 bash -- -c \
  'for i in /config/*/*; do echo $i; cat -n $i; echo ; done'
/config/cpu/limits
     1  1000
/config/cpu/requests
     1  500
/config/cpu/value
     1  4000
/config/memory/limits
     1  1073741824
/config/memory/requests
     1  524288000
/config/memory/value
     1  17179869184
```

CHAPTER 7

Scaling an Application

We have seen in the spec of the `ReplicaSet` and `Deployment` a `replicas` field. This field indicates how many replicas of a Pod should be running.

Manual Scaling

In declarative form, it is possible to edit the spec of the Deployment to change the value of this field:

```
apiVersion: apps/v1 kind:
Deployment
metadata:
  name: nginx
  labels:
    app: nginx
spec:
  replicas: 4
  selector:
    matchLabels:
      app: nginx
  template:
    metadata:
      labels:
        app: nginx
```

© Philippe Martin 2021
P. Martin, *Kubernetes*, https://doi.org/10.1007/978-1-4842-6494-2_7

```
spec:
  containers:
  - image:  nginx
    name: nginx
```

In imperative form, the command kubectl scale is used to change this value:

```
$ kubectl create deployment nginx --image=nginx
deployment.apps/nginx created
$ kubectl scale deployment nginx --replicas=4
deployment.apps/nginx scaled
```

Auto-scaling

The HorizontalPodAutoscaler resource (commonly called **HPA**) can be used to scale Deployments automatically depending on the CPU usage of the current replicas.

HPA depends on the installation of the Kubernetes Metrics Server[1] on the cluster.

To install it, run:

```
$ kubectl apply -f https://github.com/kubernetes-sigs/metrics-server/releases/download/v0.3.7/components.yaml
```

You have to edit the metrics-server Deployment in order to add the --kubelet-insecure-tls and --kubelet-preferred-address-types=InternalIP flags to the command started in the container, and to add hostNetwork: true:

---

[1]https://github.com/kubernetes-sigs/metrics-server

```
$ kubectl edit deployment metrics-server -n kube-system

    spec:
      hostNetwork: true ## add this line
      containers:
      - args:
        - --cert-dir=/tmp
        - --secure-port=4443
        - --kubelet-insecure-tls # add this line
        - --kubelet-preferred-address-types=InternalIP ## add
            this line
```

You can examine the status of the v1beta1.metrics.k8s.io
APIService with:

```
$ kubectl get apiservice v1beta1.metrics.k8s.io -o yaml
[...]
status:
  conditions:
  - lastTransitionTime: "2020-08-15T15:38:44Z"
    message: all checks passed
    reason: Passed
    status: "True"
    type: Available
```

You should now get results from the following command:

```
$ kubectl top nodes
NAME          CPU(cores)   CPU%   MEMORY(bytes)   MEMORY%
Controller    95m          9%     1256Mi              34%
worker-0      34m          3%     902Mi               25%
worker-1      30m          3%     964Mi               26%
```

You can now start a Deployment with a single replica. Note that a CPU resource request is necessary for HPA to work:

```
$ kubectl create deployment nginx --image=nginx
deployment.apps/nginx created
$ kubectl set resources --requests=cpu=0.05 deployment/nginx
deployment.extensions/nginx resource requirements updated
```

Create now a HorizontalPodAutoscaler resource for this Deployment that will be able to auto-scale the Deployment from one to four replicas, with a CPU utilization of 5%, in imperative form:

```
$ kubectl autoscale deployment nginx \
--min=1 --max=4 --cpu-percent=5
horizontalpodautoscaler.autoscaling/nginx autoscaled
```

or in declarative form:

```
apiVersion: autoscaling/v1
kind: HorizontalPodAutoscaler
metadata:
  name: nginx
spec:
  minReplicas: 1
  maxReplicas: 4
  scaleTargetRef:
    apiVersion: apps/v1
    kind: Deployment
    name: nginx
  targetCPUUtilizationPercentage: 5
```

To augment the CPU utilization of the Pod currently running, you can use the curl command to make a lot of requests on it:

```
$ kubectl get pods
NAME                        READY   STATUS    RESTARTS   AGE
nginx-xxxxxxxxxx-yyyyy       1/1     Running   0          31s
$ kubectl port-forward pod/nginx-xxxxxxxxxx-yyyyy 8084:80
Forwarding from 127.0.0.1:8084 -> 80
```

and in another terminal:

$ while : ; **do** curl http://localhost:8084; **done**

In parallel, you can follow the utilization of CPU by the Pod with the command:

```
$ kubectl top pods
NAME                        CPU(cores)   MEMORY(bytes)
nginx-xxxxxxxxxx-yyyyy      3m           2Mi
```

Once the CPU utilization becomes more than 5%, a second Pod will be automatically deployed:

```
$ kubectl get hpa nginx
NAME     REFERENCE
TARGETS   MINPODS    MAXPODS    REPLICAS
nginx    Deployment/nginx   7%/5%       1           4            2
```

```
$ kubectl get pods
NAME                        READY   STATUS    RESTARTS   AGE
nginx-5c55b4d6c8-fgnlz      1/1     Running   0          12m
nginx-5c55b4d6c8-hzgfl      1/1     Running   0          81s
```

If you stop the curl requests and watch the created HPA, you can see that the number of replicas will be set to 1 again 5 minutes after the CPU utilization is low again:

```
$ kubectl get hpa nginx -w
```

NAME	REFERENCE	TARGETS	MINPODS	MAXPODS	REPLICAS	AGE
nginx	Deployment/nginx	4%/5%	1	4	2	10m
nginx	Deployment/nginx	3%/5%	1	4	2	10m
nginx	Deployment/nginx	0%/5%	1	4	2	11m
nginx	Deployment/nginx	0%/5%	1	4	1	16m

And you can examine the events created by the HPA:

```
$ kubectl describe hpa nginx
[...]
Events:
  Type    Reason             Age From                       Message
  ----    ------             --- ----                       -------
  Normal SuccessfulRescale 10m horizontal-pod-autoscaler New
  size: 2; reason: \
cpu resource utilization (percentage of request) above target
  Normal SuccessfulRescale 2m47s horizontal-pod-autoscaler New
size: 1; reason: \
All metrics below target
```

CHAPTER 8

Application Self-Healing

When you start a Pod on a cluster, it is scheduled on a specific node of the cluster. If the node, at a given moment, is not able to continue to host this Pod, the Pod will not be restarted on a new node – the application is not self-healing.

Let's have a try, on a cluster with more than one worker (e.g., on the cluster installed in Chapter 1).

First, run a Pod; then examine on which node it has been scheduled:

```
$ kubectl run nginx --image=nginx
pod/nginx created
$ kubectl get pods -o wide
NAME    READY   STATUS    RESTARTS   AGE   IP           NODE
nginx   1/1     Running   0          12s   10.244.1.8   worker-0
```

Here, the Pod has been scheduled on the node worker-0.

Let's put this node in maintenance mode, to see what happens to the Pod:

```
$ kubectl drain worker-0 --force
node/worker-0 cordoned
WARNING: deleting Pods not managed by ReplicationController,
ReplicaSet, Job, Daemon\
Set or StatefulSet: default/nginx
```

© Philippe Martin 2021
P. Martin, *Kubernetes*, https://doi.org/10.1007/978-1-4842-6494-2_8

```
evicting pod "nginx"
pod/nginx evicted
node/worker-0 evicted
$ kubectl get pods
No resources found in default namespace.
```

You can see that the Pod you created has disappeared and has not been recreated in another node. We finish our experiment here. You can make your node schedulable again:

```
$ kubectl uncordon worker-0
node/worker-0 uncordoned
```

Controller to the Rescue

We have seen in Chapter 5, section "Pod Controllers," that using Pod controllers ensures your Pod is scheduled in another node if one node stops to work.

Let's make the experience again, with a Deployment:

```
$ kubectl create deployment nginx --image=nginx
deployment.apps/nginx created
$ kubectl get pods -o wide
NAME                      READY   STATUS    RESTARTS   AGE   IP
NODE
nginx-554b9c67f9-ndtsz    1/1     Running   0
11s   10.244.1.9 worker-0
$ kubectl drain worker-0
node/worker-0 cordoned
evicting pod "nginx-554b9c67f9-ndtsz"
pod/nginx-554b9c67f9-ndtsz evicted
node/worker-0 evicted
```

```
$ kubectl get pods -o wide
NAME                      READY   STATUS   RESTARTS   AGE
   IP            NODE
nginx-554b9c67f9-5kz5v    1/1     Running  0          4s
   10.244.2.9    worker-1
```

This time, we can see that a Pod has been recreated in another node of the cluster – our app now survives a node eviction.

Liveness Probes

It is possible to define a liveness probe for each container of a Pod. If the kubelet is not able to execute the probe successfully a given number of times, the container is considered not healthy and is restarted into the same Pod.

This probe should be used to detect that the container is not responsive.

There are three possibilities for the liveness probe:

- Make an HTTP request.

  If your container is an HTTP server, you can add an endpoint that always replies with a success response and define the probe with this endpoint. If your backend is not healthy anymore, it is probable that this endpoint will not respond either.

- Execute a command.

  Most server applications have an associate CLI application. You can use this CLI to execute a very simple operation on the server. If the server is not healthy, it is probable it will not respond to this simple request either.

- Make a TCP connection.

  When a server running in a container communicates via a non-HTTP protocol (on top of TCP), you can try to open a socket to the application. If the server is not healthy, it is probable that it will not respond to this connection request.

You have to use the declarative form to declare liveness probes.

A Note About Readiness Probes

Note that it is also possible to define a **readiness probe** for a container. The main role of the readiness probe is to indicate if a Pod is ready to serve network requests. The Pod will be added to the list of backends of matching Services when the readiness probe succeeds.

Later, during the container execution, if a readiness probe fails, the Pod will be removed from the list of backends of Services. This can be useful to detect that a container is not able to handle more connections (e.g., if it is already treating a lot of connections) and stop sending new ones.

HTTP Request Liveness Probe

```
apiVersion: v1
kind: Pod
metadata:
  name: nginx
spec:
  containers:
  - image: nginx
    name: nginx
```

```
livenessProbe:
  httpGet:
    scheme: HTTP
    port: 80
    path: /healthz
```

Here, we define a probe that queries the /healthz endpoint. As **nginx** is not configured by default to reply to this path, it will reply with a 404 response code, and the probe will fail. This is not a real case, but that simulates an nginx server that would reply in error to a simple request.

You can see in the Pod events that after three failed probes, the container is restarted:

```
$ kubectl describe pod nginx
[...]
Events:
  Type      Reason      Age                   From
Message
  ----      ------      ----                  ----
-------
  Normal    Started     31s                   kubelet, minikube
Started container nginx
  Normal    Pulling     0s (x2 over 33s)   kubelet, minikube
Pulling image "nginx"
  Warning   Unhealthy   0s (x3 over 20s)   kubelet, minikube
Liveness probe failed: HTTP probe failed with statuscode: 404
  Normal    Killing     0s                    kubelet, minikube
Container nginx failed liveness probe, will be restarted
```

Command Liveness Probe

```
apiVersion: v1
kind: Pod
metadata:
  name: postgres
spec:
  containers:
  - image: postgres
    name: postgres
    livenessProbe:
      initialDelaySeconds: 10
      exec:
        command:
        - "psql"
        - "-h"
        - "localhost"
        - "-U"
        - "unknownUser"
        - "-c"
        - "select 1"
```

Here, the liveness probe tries to connect to the server using the psql command and execute a very simple SQL query (SELECT 1) as user unknownUser. As this user does not exist, the query will fail.

You can see in the Pod events that after three failed probes, the container is restarted:

```
$ kubectl describe pod postgres
[...]
Events:
  Type      Reason     Age                 From
Message
  ----      ------     ----                ----
-------
  Normal    Scheduled  <unknown>                  default-
scheduler  Successfully assigned default/postgres to minikube
  Warning   Unhealthy  0s (x3 over 20s)           kubelet,
minikube  Liveness probe failed: psql: error: could not connect
to server: FATAL: role "unknownUser" does not exist
  Normal    Killing    0s                         kubelet,
minikube  Container postgres failed liveness probe, will be
restarted
```

TCP Connection Liveness Probe

```
apiVersion: v1
kind: Pod
metadata:
  name: postgres
spec:
  containers:
  - image: postgres
    name: postgres
    livenessProbe:
      initialDelaySeconds: 10
      tcpSocket:
        port: 5433
```

Here, the liveness probe tries to connect to the container on the 5433 port. As postgres listens on the port 5432, the connection will fail.

You can see in the Pod events that after three failed probes, the container is restarted:

```
$ kubectl describe pod postgres
[...]
Events:
  Type      Reason      Age                 From
Message
  ----      ------      ----                ----
-------
  Normal    Started     25s                 kubelet, minikube
Started container postgres
  Warning   Unhealthy   0s (x3 over 15s)    kubelet, minikube
Liveness probe failed: dial tcp 172.17.0.3:5433: connect:
connection refused
  Normal    Killing     0s                  kubelet,
minikube   Container postgres failed  liveness probe, will be
restarted
```

Resource Limits and Quality of Service (QoS) Classes

You can define for each container of Pods resource (CPU and memory) requests and limits.

The resource requests values are used to schedule a Pod in a node having at least the requested resources available (see Chapter 9, section "Resource Requests").

If you do not declare limits, each container will still have access to all the resources of the node; in this case, if some Pods are not using all their requested resources at a given time, some other containers will be able to use them and vice versa.

In contrast, if a limit is declared for a container, the container will be constrained to those particular resources. If it tries to allocate more memory than its limit, it will get a memory allocation error and will probably crash or work on a degraded mode; and it will have access to the CPU in its limit only.

Depending on whether the requests and limits values are declared or not, a different Quality of Service is assured for a Pod:

- If all containers of a Pod have declared requests and limits for all resources (CPU and memory) and the limits equal the requests, the Pod will be running with a *Guaranteed* QoS class.

- Or if at least one container of a Pod has a resource request or limit, the Pod will be running with a *Burstable* QoS class.

- Otherwise, if no request nor limit is declared for its containers, the Pod will be running with a *Best Effort* QoS class.

If a node runs out of an incompressible resource (memory), the associated kubelet can decide to eject one or more Pods, to prevent total starvation of the resource.

The Pods evicted are decided depending on their Quality of Service class: first *Best Effort* ones, then *Burstable* ones, and finally *Guaranteed* ones.

CHAPTER 9

Scheduling Pods

When you want to run a Pod into a Kubernetes cluster, you generally do not specify on which node you want the Pod to run. This is the job of the Kubernetes scheduler to determine on which node it will be running.

The Pod specs contain a `nodeName` field indicating on which node the Pod is scheduled.

The scheduler perpetually watches for Pods; when it finds a Pod with an empty `nodeName` field, the scheduler determines the best node on which to schedule this Pod and then modifies the Pod spec to write the `nodeName` field with the selected node.

In parallel, the kubelet components, affected to specific nodes, watch the Pods; when a Pod marked with a `nodeName` matches the node of a kubelet, the Pod is affected to the kubelet, which deploys it to its node.

Using Label Selectors to Schedule Pods on Specific Nodes

The Pod spec contains a `nodeSelector` field, as a map of key-value pairs. When set, the Pod is deployable only on nodes having each key-value pair as label.

The typical usage is that nodes have some labels indicating some specificities, and when you want to deploy a Pod on a node having a specificity, you add the corresponding label to the `nodeSelector` field of the Pod.

© Philippe Martin 2021
P. Martin, *Kubernetes*, https://doi.org/10.1007/978-1-4842-6494-2_9

Adding Labels to Nodes

The first step is to add labels to nodes. Consider you have four nodes, two with SSD disks and two with HDD disks. You can label the nodes with the commands:

```
$ kubectl label node worker-0 disk=ssd
node/worker-0 labeled
$ kubectl label node worker-1 disk=ssd
node/worker-1 labeled
$ kubectl label node worker-2 disk=hdd
node/worker-2 labeled
$ kubectl label node worker-3 disk=hdd
node/worker-3 labeled
```

Among these nodes, two provide GPU units. Let's label them:

```
$ kubectl label node worker-0 compute=gpu
node/worker-0 labeled
$ kubectl label node worker-2 compute=gpu
node/worker-1 labeled
```

Adding Node Selectors to Pods

Imagine you want to deploy a Pod that needs an SSD disk. You can create this Deployment. The Pod will be schedulable on worker-0 and worker-1:

```
apiVersion: apps/v1
kind: Deployment
metadata:
  labels:
    app: nginx
  name: nginx
```

```
spec:
  replicas: 1
  selector:
    matchLabels:
      app: nginx
  template:
    metadata:
      labels:
        app: nginx
    spec:
      nodeSelector:
        disk: ssd
      containers:
      - image: nginx
        name: nginx
```

Now, if the Pod needs an SSD disk **and** a GPU unit, you can create this Deployment. The Pod will be schedulable on worker-0 only:

```
apiVersion: apps/v1
kind: Deployment
metadata:
  labels:
    app: nginx
  name: nginx
spec:
  replicas: 1
  selector:
    matchLabels:
      app: nginx
  template:
    metadata:
```

```
    labels:
      app: nginx
  spec:
    nodeSelector:
      disk: ssd
      compute: gpu
    containers:
    - image: nginx
      name: nginx
```

Manual Scheduling

Remember, the Kubernetes scheduler looks for Pods with empty nodeName and kubelet components look for Pods with their associated node name.

If you create a Pod and specify yourself the nodeName in its spec, the scheduler will never see it, and the associated kubelet will adopt it immediately. The effect is that the Pod will be scheduled on the specified node, without the help of the scheduler.

DaemonSets

The DaemonSet Kubernetes resource guarantees that all (or a given subset of) nodes run a copy of a given Pod.

The typical use of a DaemonSet is to deploy daemons (storage daemons, logs daemons, monitoring daemons) on every node of a cluster.

Because of this particularity, the Pods created by DaemonSets are not scheduled by the Kubernetes scheduler, but by the DaemonSet controller itself.

The spec of a DaemonSet is similar to a Deployment spec, with these differences:

- The DaemonSet spec does not contain a `replicas` field, as this quantity is given by the number of selected nodes.

- The `strategy` field of the Deployment is replaced by an `updateStrategy` field in the DaemonSet.

- The `progressDeadlineSeconds` and `paused` fields are absent from the DaemonSet spec.

By default, the DaemonSet will deploy Pods on every node of the cluster. If you want to select a subset of nodes only, you can use the `nodeSelector` field of the Pod spec to select the nodes by label, as you would do for a Deployment (see Chapter 9, section "Using label selectors to schedule Pods on specific nodes").

As an example, here is a DaemonSet that would deploy a hypothetical GPU daemon on nodes labeled with `compute=gpu`:

```yaml
apiVersion: apps/v1
kind: DaemonSet
metadata:
  name: gpu-daemon
  labels:
    app: gpu-daemon
spec:
  selector:
    matchLabels:
      app: gpu-daemon
  template:
    metadata:
      labels:
        app: gpu-daemon
```

```
spec:
  nodeSelector:
    compute: gpu
  containers:
  - image: gpu-daemon
    name: gpu-daemon
```

Static Pods

Static Pods are directly attached to a kubelet daemon. They are declared in files located on the host of the node running the kubelet daemon, in a specific directory.

You can find the directory in the kubelet configuration file, under the staticPodPath field.

The configuration of a kubelet is accessible via the Kubernetes API, at the following path: /api/v1/nodes/<node-name>/proxy/configz.

To access the API easily, you can run the kubectl proxy command:

```
$ kubectl proxy
Starting to serve on 127.0.0.1:8001
```

You now have access to the API on http://127.0.0.1:8001, with the same rights you have with kubectl.

Now in another terminal, you can execute the curl command to get the configuration of the kubelet daemon on the worker-0 node:

```
$ curl "http://localhost:8001/api/v1/nodes/worker-0/proxy/
configz" \
  | python -m json.tool
{
    "kubeletconfig": {
        "staticPodPath": "/etc/kubernetes/manifests",
```

```
[...]
    }
}
```

You can now create a manifest to declare a Pod on this directory, on the worker-0 host:

```
$ gcloud compute ssh worker-0
Welcome to Ubuntu 18.04.3 LTS
$ cat <<EOF | sudo tee /etc/kubernetes/manifests/nginx.yaml
apiVersion: v1
kind: Pod
metadata:
  name: nginx
spec:
  containers:
  - image: nginx
    name: nginx
EOF
```

Back to your developer machine, you can see that the Pod appears in the list of the running Pods and that kubelet suffixed the name of the Pod with the name of the node:

```
$ kubectl get pods
NAME            READY   STATUS    RESTARTS   AGE
nginx-worker-0   1/1     Running   0          11s
```

If you delete the Pod, it will be immediately recreated by kubelet:

```
$ kubectl delete pod nginx-worker-0
pod "nginx-worker-0" deleted
$ kubectl get pods
NAME            READY   STATUS    RESTARTS   AGE
nginx-worker-0   0/1     Pending   0          1s
```

When you remove the manifest from the worker-0 host, the Pod will be immediately deleted by kubelet.

```
$ gcloud compute ssh worker-0
Welcome to Ubuntu 18.04.3 LTS
$ sudo rm /etc/kubernetes/manifests/nginx.yaml
```

Resource Requests

Each node has a maximum capacity of CPU and memory. Each time a Pod is scheduled on a node, the CPU and memory amounts requested by this Pod are removed from the CPU and memory available on this node.

A Pod cannot be scheduled on a node if the available resources on this node are less than the amounts requested by this Pod.

For this reason, it is very important to declare resource requests for **all** the Pods you deploy. Otherwise, the computation of the available resources would be inaccurate.

In Imperative Form

The kubectl set resources command is used to set resource requests on an object (here a Deployment):

```
$ kubectl create deployment nginx --image=nginx
deployment.apps/nginx created
$ kubectl set resources deployment nginx \
  --requests=cpu=0.1,memory=1Gi
deployment.extensions/nginx resource requirements updated
```

In Declarative Form

You can declare resource requests for each container of a Pod, using the resources field of the Container spec:

```
apiVersion: apps/v1
kind: Deployment
metadata:
  labels:
    app: nginx
  name: nginx
spec:
  selector:
    matchLabels:
      app: nginx
  template:
    metadata:
      labels:
        app: nginx
    spec:
      containers:
      - image: nginx
        name: nginx
        resources:
          requests:
            cpu: 100m
            memory: 1Gi
```

Running Multiple Schedulers

Kubernetes is shipped with a default scheduler and gives you the possibility to run your own schedulers in parallel. In that case, when you create a Pod, you will be able to select the scheduler you want to be used for this Pod.

You can get an example scheduler on the feloy/scheduler-round-robin GitHub repository.[1]

The code of this scheduler is simplistic and must not be used in production, but demonstrates the lifecycle of a scheduler:

- Listening for Pods without a nodeName value

- Selecting a node

- Binding the selected node to the Pod

- Sending an event

Once this new scheduler is deployed in your cluster (please follow the instructions in the repository), you can verify that the scheduler has found the workers of the cluster:

```
$ kubectl logs scheduler-round-robin-xxxxxxxxxx-yyyyy -f
found 2 nodes: [worker-0 worker-1]
```

You can now create a Deployment specifying this specific scheduler:

```
apiVersion: apps/v1
kind: Deployment
metadata:
  labels:
    app: nginx
  name: nginx
```

---

[1]https://github.com/feloy/scheduler-round-robin

```
spec:
  replicas: 4
  selector:
    matchLabels:
      app: nginx
  template:
    metadata:
      labels:
        app: nginx
    spec:
      schedulerName: scheduler-round-robin
      containers:
      - image: nginx
        name: nginx
```

Using the command kubectl get pods -o wide, you can see that two Pods have been deployed in worker-0 and two in worker-1.

Examine Scheduler Events

If you look at the events attached to a deployed Pod, you can see that the Pod has been scheduled by the scheduler-round-robin scheduler:

```
$ kubectl describe pod nginx-xxxxxxxxxx-yyyyy
[...]
Events:
  Type    Reason     Age   From                    Message
  ----    ------     ----  ----                    -------
  Normal  Scheduled  30s   scheduler-round-robin   pod nginx-
                                                   6dcb7cd47-
                                                   9c9w5
                                                   schedule\
d to node worker-0
```

You can go through all the events to find the events created by schedulers:

```
$ kubectl get events | grep Scheduled
0s              Normal      Scheduled
pod/nginx-554b9c67f9-snpkb          \
          Successfully assigned default/nginx-554b9c67f9-snpkb
          to worker-0
```

## CHAPTER 10

Discovery and Load Balancing

When you deploy a Pod, it is not easily accessible. If you define a Pod with several containers, these containers will be available to communicate via the localhost interface, but containers of a Pod won't be able to communicate with containers of another Pod without knowing the IP address of the other Pod.

But the Pod is volatile. We have seen that a Pod by itself is not usable because it can be evicted from a node at any time and won't be recreated automatically. Controllers like `ReplicaSet` are necessary to guarantee that a given number of replicas of a Pod are running. In this case, even if you get the IP address of a Pod, it is not guaranteed that this Pod survives, and the next one won't have the same IP address of the first one.

Services

The `Service` Kubernetes resource is used to make a Pod accessible via the network in a reproducible way.

In imperative form, you can use the `kubectl expose` command:

```
$ kubectl create deployment nginx --image=nginx
deployment.apps/nginx created
$ kubectl expose deployment nginx --port 80
service/webapp exposed
```

© Philippe Martin 2021
P. Martin, *Kubernetes*, https://doi.org/10.1007/978-1-4842-6494-2_10

```
$ kubectl get services
NAME          TYPE          CLUSTER-IP       EXTERNAL-IP    PORT(S)    AGE
webapp        ClusterIP     10.97.68.130     <none>         80/TCP     5s
```

In declarative form, you can create the Service with this template:

```
apiVersion: v1
kind: Service
metadata:
  name: webapp
spec:
  ports:
  - port: 80
  selector:
    app: nginx
```

Now, we can try to deploy another Pod, connect to it, and try to communicate with this nginx Pod:

```
$ kubectl run \
  --image=busybox box \
   sh -- -c 'sleep $((10**10))'
pod/box created
$ kubectl exec -it box sh
/ # wget http://webapp -q -O -
<!DOCTYPE html>
<html> [...]
</html>
/ # exit
```

Selectors

You have seen with the previous examples that a Service makes a Pod accessible. More generally, a Service is a frontend for a list of **backend** Pods. This list of backend Pods is determined by the `selector` field of the `Service` resource; all the Pods with keys and values as labels matching this selector are eligible to be part of the list of backends.

Readiness Probes

Once the list of Pods eligible to be a backend of a Service is determined by the `selector` field, the readiness of the Pods is also taken into account. The Pod is effectively inserted in the list of backends when the Pod is in the **Ready** state.

The Pod is considered ready when all its containers are ready, and a container is ready either when it does not define a `readinessProbe` or when its `readinessProbe` succeeds.

Note that this readiness is considered when the Pod starts, but also during all the life of the Pod. At any time, a container can declare itself not ready (e.g., because it thinks it is not able to handle more requests), and the Pod will be immediately removed from the list of backends of matching Services.

Endpoints

The effective backends of a `Service` are materialized by the `Endpoints` resource. The Endpoints controller is in charge of creating and deleting endpoints, depending on the readiness of Pods and selectors of Services.

You can see the list of endpoints for a Service (here `nginx`) with the command

```
$ kubectl get endpoints nginx
NAME     ENDPOINTS                          AGE
nginx    172.17.0.10:80,172.17.0.9:80 7m    48s
```

In this case, the Service has two endpoints, and the traffic for the Service will be routed to these two endpoints.

You can get the details of the two endpoints. Here, you see that the two endpoints are the two Pods `nginx-86c57db685-g4fqr` and `nginx-86c57db685-9hp58`:

```
$ kubectl get endpoints nginx -o yaml
apiVersion: v1
kind: Endpoints
metadata:
  labels:
    app: nginx
  name: nginx
  [...]
subsets:
- addresses:
  - ip: 172.17.0.10
    nodeName: minikube
    targetRef:
      kind: Pod
      name: nginx-86c57db685-g4fqr
      namespace: default
      resourceVersion: "621228"
      uid: adb2d120-14ed-49ad-b9a5-4389412b73b1
  - ip: 172.17.0.9
    nodeName: minikube
```

```
    targetRef:
      kind: Pod
      name: nginx-86c57db685-9hp58
      namespace: default
      resourceVersion: "621169"
      uid: 5b051d79-9951-4ca9-a436-5dbe3f46169b
ports:
- port: 80
  protocol: TCP
```

Service Types

ClusterIP

By default, the Service is created with the `ClusterIP` type. With this type, the Service is accessible from inside the cluster only.

An IP address local to the cluster will be reserved for this Service, and a DNS entry will be created that points to this address, under the form `<name>.<namespace>.svc.cluster.local`, in our example `webapp.default.svc.cluster.local`.

If you examine the `resolv.conf` file inside a container, you see that the search entry indicates:

```
$ kubectl exec -it box cat /etc/resolv.conf
nameserver 10.96.0.10
search default.svc.cluster.local svc.cluster.local cluster.local
```

Thanks to this, from inside a Pod, you can access a Service defined in the namespace with its name only (here `webapp`) or its name.namespace (here `webapp.default`) or its name.namespace.svc (here `webapp.default.svc`) or its complete name (`webapp.default.svc.cluster.local`).

To access a Service defined in another namespace, you will have to specify at least the name and namespace (e.g., `another-app.other-namespace`).

NodePort

If you want to access a Service from outside the cluster, you can use the `NodePort` type. In addition to creating a ClusterIP, this will allocate a port (in the range 30000–32767 by default) on every node of the cluster, which will route to the ClusterIP.

LoadBalancer

If you want to access a Service from outside the cloud environment, you can use the `LoadBalancer` type. In addition to creating a `NodePort`, it will create an external load balancer (if you use a managed Kubernetes cluster like Google GKE, Azure AKS, Amazon EKS, etc.), which routes to the ClusterIP via the `NodePort`.

ExternalName

This is a specific type of Service, where the `selector` field is not used and the Service redirects instead to an external DNS name, using a DNS `CNAME` record.

Ingress

With a LoadBalancer Service, you can access a microservice of your application. If you have several applications, each with several access points (at least frontend and API), you will need to reserve lots of load balancers, which can be very costly.

An Ingress is equivalent to an Apache or nginx **virtual host**; it permits to multiplex access points to several microservices into a single load balancer. The selection is done on the hostname and path of the request.

You have to install an **Ingress controller** in your cluster in order to use Ingress resources.

Install nginx Ingress Controller

You can follow the installation instructions.[1] In summary, you have to execute

```
$ kubectl apply -f https://raw.githubusercontent.com/
kubernetes/ingress-nginx/controller-v0.34.1/deploy/static/
provider/baremetal/deploy.yaml
[...]
```

Get the ports on which the Ingress controller listens for external connections, in this case the ports *32351* (mapped to port 80) and *31296* (mapped to 443), and store them on environment variables for later use:

```
$ kubectl get services -n ingress-nginx
NAME            TYPE       CLUSTER-IP       EXTERNAL-IP    PORT(S)    \
    AGE
ingress-nginx   NodePort   10.100.169.243   <none>         80:32351/TCP,
                                                           443:31296/TCP\
    9h
$ HTTP_PORT=32351
$ HTTPS_PORT=31296
```

Note that the ingress-nginx Service is of type NodePort; the Service will be accessible on each worker of the cluster, on ports 32351 (for HTTP connections) and 31296 (for HTTPS connections).

---

[1]https://kubernetes.github.io/ingress-nginx/deploy/

We have to add a firewall rule that enables the traffic on these ports on the worker VMs:

```
$ gcloud compute firewall-rules create \
  kubernetes-cluster-allow-external-ingress \
  --allow tcp:$HTTP_PORT,tcp:$HTTPS_PORT \
  --network kubernetes-cluster \
  --source-ranges 0.0.0.0/0
```

Get the public IP address of the first worker:

```
$ WORKER_IP=$(gcloud compute instances describe worker-0 \
  --zone $(gcloud config get-value compute/zone) \
  --format='get(networkInterfaces[0].accessConfigs[0].natIP)')
```

From your local computer, you can try to connect to these ports:

```
$ curl http://$WORKER_IP:$HTTP_PORT
<html>
<head><title>404 Not Found</title></head>
<body>
<center><h1>404 Not Found</h1></center>
<hr><center>nginx/1.17.7</center>
</body>
</html>
$ curl -k https://$WORKER_IP:$HTTPS_PORT
<html>
<head><title>404 Not Found</title></head>
<body>
<center><h1>404 Not Found</h1></center>
<hr><center>nginx/1.17.7</center>
</body>
</html>
```

If you can see these responses, the Ingress controller is running correctly, and you are redirected to the default backend that returns 404 errors.

Accessing Applications

Now, let's create a simple application (an Apache server) and expose it via an Ingress resource:

```
$ kubectl create deployment webapp --image=httpd
deployment.apps/webapp created
$ kubectl expose deployment webapp --port 80
service/webapp exposed
$ kubectl apply -f - <<EOF
apiVersion: extensions/v1beta1
kind: Ingress
metadata:
  name: webapp-ingress
spec:
  backend:
    serviceName: webapp
    servicePort: 80
EOF
```

With this Ingress configuration, all the requests to the Ingress controller will be routed to the webapp Service:

```
$ curl http://$WORKER_IP:$HTTP_PORT/
<html><body><h1>It works!</h1></body></html>
```

Now, let's multiplex several applications on the same Ingress, by deploying a second web application, this time the kennship/http-echo image:

```
$ kubectl create deployment echo --image=kennship/http-echo
deployment.apps/echo created
$ kubectl expose deployment echo --port 3000
service/echo exposed
$ kubectl delete ingress webapp-ingress
ingress.extensions "webapp-ingress" deleted
$ kubectl apply -f - <<EOF
apiVersion: extensions/v1beta1
kind: Ingress
metadata:
  name: plex-ingress
spec:
  rules:
  - host: webapp.com
    http:
      paths:
      - path: /
        backend:
          serviceName: webapp
          servicePort: 80
  - host: echo.com
    http:
      paths:
      - path: /
        backend:
          serviceName: echo
          servicePort: 3000
EOF
```

We can now access the different applications by using their hostnames:

```
$ curl -H 'Host: echo.com' http://$WORKER_IP:$HTTP_PORT/
{"path":"/","headers":{"host":"echo.com","x-request-id":"350237
1d3a479598bc393aa61a8\
b6896","x-real-ip":"10.240.0.20","x-forwarded-
for":"10.240.0.20","x-forwarded-host":\
"echo.com","x-forwarded-port":"80","x-forwarded-
proto":"http","x-scheme":"http","use\
r-agent":"curl/7.58.0","accept":"*/*"},"method":"GET",
"body":{},"fresh":false,"hostn\
ame":"echo.com","ip":"::ffff:10.244.1.49","ips":[],
"protocol":"http","query":{},"sub\
domains":[],"xhr":false}

$ curl -H 'Host: webapp.com' http://$WORKER_IP:$HTTP_PORT/
<html><body><h1>It works!</h1></body></html>
```

HTTPS and Ingress

If you try to connect using HTTPS protocol, on the HTTPS port of the Ingress controller (here 31296), you can see that the Ingress controller is using a fake certificate:

```
$ curl -k -v -H 'Host: webapp.com' https://$WORKER_IP:$HTTPS_
PORT/
[...]
* Server certificate:
*   subject: O=Acme Co; CN=Kubernetes Ingress Controller Fake
    Certificate
*   start date: Jan 17 16:59:01 2020 GMT
```

```
*  expire date: Jan 16 16:59:01 2021 GMT
*  issuer: O=Acme Co; CN=Kubernetes Ingress Controller Fake
   Certificate
[...]
```

Let's use our own certificate, in this example an auto-generated one, but the procedure would be the same with a signed one. First, generate the certificate, and then create a tls secret containing the certificate:

```
$ openssl req -x509 -nodes -days 365 -newkey rsa:2048 \
    -out echo-ingress-tls.crt \
    -keyout echo-ingress-tls.key \
    -subj "/CN=echo.com/O=echo-ingress-tls"
[...]
$ kubectl create secret tls echo-ingress-tls \
    --key echo-ingress-tls.key \
    --cert echo-ingress-tls.crt
secret/echo-ingress-tls created
```

Then add a section to the Ingress resource:

```
apiVersion: extensions/v1beta1
kind: Ingress
metadata:
  name: plex-ingress
spec:
  tls:
  - hosts:
    - echo.com
    secretName: echo-ingress-tls
  rules:
  - host: webapp.com
    http:
      paths:
```

```
      - path: /
        backend:
          serviceName: webapp
          servicePort: 80
  - host: echo.com
    http:
      paths:
      - path: /
        backend:
          serviceName: echo
          servicePort: 3000
```

With these changes, the echo.com requests will now use this new certificate:

```
$ curl -k -v --resolve echo.com:$HTTPS_PORT:$WORKER_IP https://
echo.com:$HTTPS_PORT/
[...]
* Server certificate:
*   subject: CN=echo.com; O=echo-ingress-tls
*   start date: Jan 17 18:10:33 2020 GMT
*   expire date: Jan 16 18:10:33 2021 GMT
*   issuer: CN=echo.com; O=echo-ingress-tls
*   SSL certificate verify result: self signed certificate (18),
continuing anyway.
[...]
```

And webapp.com will still use the default one:

```
$ curl -k -v --resolve webapp.com:$HTTPS_PORT:$WORKER_IP
https://webapp.com:$HTTPS_PORT
[...]
```

```
* Server certificate:
*   subject: O=Acme Co; CN=Kubernetes Ingress Controller Fake
    Certificate
*   start date: Jan 17 16:59:01 2020 GMT
*   expire date: Jan 16 16:59:01 2021 GMT
*   issuer: O=Acme Co; CN=Kubernetes Ingress Controller Fake
    Certificate
[...]
```

CHAPTER 11

Security

Kubernetes is a secured system: you first need to be authenticated, as a normal user or as a service account; then, an authorization system validates that you have the rights to perform the requested operations.

Moreover, it is possible to limit the rights of containers on the host system by defining security contexts and limit the rights of containers in the network by defining network policies.

Authentication

Kubernetes defines two kinds of users: **normal users** and **service accounts**.

Normal User Authentication

Normal users are not managed by the Kubernetes API. You must have an external system managing users and their credentials. Authentication for normal users can be handled by different methods:

- Client Certificate
- HTTP Basic Auth
- Bearer Token
- Authentication proxy

© Philippe Martin 2021
P. Martin, *Kubernetes*, https://doi.org/10.1007/978-1-4842-6494-2_11

Client Certificate Authentication

When using kubeadm to install a cluster, the API server is configured with the option

```
--client-ca-file=/etc/kubernetes/pki/ca.crt
```

This option is necessary for the cluster to enable Client Certificate authentication. The ca.crt contains the certificate authority.

For a new user, the first step for the user is to create a certificate signing request (CSR):

```
# Create a private key
$ openssl genrsa -out user.key 4096
[...]
```

Create the csr.cnf configuration file to generate the CSR:

```
[ req ]
default_bits = 2048
prompt = no
default_md = sha256
distinguished_name = dn

[ dn ]
CN = user
O = company

[ v3_ext ]
authorityKeyIdentifier=keyid,issuer:always
basicConstraints=CA:FALSE
keyUsage=keyEncipherment,dataEncipherment
extendedKeyUsage=serverAuth,clientAuth
```

Create the CSR:

```
$ openssl req -config ./csr.cnf -new -key user.key -nodes -out
user.csr
```

Second, an admin of the cluster has to sign the CSR using the
CertificateSigningRequest resource provided by the Kubernetes API:

```
# Write user CSR as base64 data
$ export CSR=$(cat user.csr | base64 | tr -d '\n')

# Create a template for the CertificateSigningRequest
$ cat > user-csr.yaml <<EOF
apiVersion: certificates.k8s.io/v1beta1
kind: CertificateSigningRequest
metadata:
  name: user-csr
spec:
  groups:
  - system:authenticated
  request: ${CSR}
  usages:
  - digital signature
  - key encipherment
  - server auth
  - client auth
EOF

# Insert CSR data into the template and apply it
$ cat user-csr.yaml | envsubst | kubectl apply -f -
certificatesigningrequest.certificates.k8s.io/user-csr created
```

```
# Verify CSR resource is created
$ kubectl get certificatesigningrequests.certificates.k8s.io
user-csr
NAME       AGE    REQUESTOR          CONDITION
user-csr   52s    kubernetes-admin   Pending

# Approve the certificate
$ kubectl certificate approve user-csr
certificatesigningrequest.certificates.k8s.io/user-csr approved

# Verify CSR is approved ans issued
$ kubectl get certificatesigningrequests.certificates.k8s.io
user-csr
NAME       AGE     REQUESTOR          CONDITION
user-csr   2m17s   kubernetes-admin   Approved,Issued

# Extract the issued certificate
$ kubectl get csr user-csr -o jsonpath='{.status.certificate}'
  | base64 --decode > user.crt
```

Third, the admin has to create a kubeconfig file for the user.

There are three parts in the kubeconfig file: server information, user information, and context information.

The command kubectl config set-cluster is used to write server information.

> Note in the following commands the presence of the
> flag --kubeconfig=userconfig. When the flag is set,
> the kubectl tool will work on this file, instead of on
> the default one ~/.kube/config:

```
$ CLUSTER_ENDPOINT=$(kubectl config view --minify --raw -o
jsonpath='{.clusters[0].cluster.server}')
$ CLUSTER_CA=$(kubectl config view --minify --raw -o
jsonpath='{.clusters[0].cluster.certificate-authority-data}')
$ echo -n $CLUSTER_CA | base64 -d > cluster.crt
$ CLUSTER_NAME=$(kubectl config view --minify --raw -o
jsonpath='{.clusters[0].name}')
$ kubectl --kubeconfig=userconfig config set-cluster $CLUSTER_
NAME \
   --server=$CLUSTER_ENDPOINT \
   --certificate-authority=cluster.crt --embed-certs
Cluster "cka" set.
```

The command kubectl config set-credentials is used to write user information:

```
$ USER_NAME=user
$ kubectl --kubeconfig=userconfig config set-credentials $USER_
NAME \
   --client-certificate=user.crt --embed-certs
User "user" set.
```

The command kubectl config set-context is used to write context information and kubectl config use-context to select the current context:

```
$ kubectl --kubeconfig=userconfig config set-context default \
   --cluster=$CLUSTER_NAME \
   --user=$USER_NAME \
   --namespace=default
Context "default" created.
$ kubectl --kubeconfig=userconfig config use-context default
Switched to context "default".
```

The admin can authorize the user to read information about nodes with these commands (more on this in the section "Authorization"):

```
$ kubectl create clusterrole nodes-read \
    --verb=get,list,watch --resource=nodes
clusterrole.rbac.authorization.k8s.io/nodes-read   created
$ kubectl create clusterrolebinding user-nodes-read \
    --clusterrole=nodes-read --user=user
clusterrolebinding.rbac.authorization.k8s.io/user-nodes-read
created
```

The admin can now send this userconfig file to the user.

The user will need to add information about their private key in the file, with the kubectl config set-credentials command:

```
$ USER_NAME=user
$ kubectl --kubeconfig=userconfig config set-credentials $USER_
NAME \
    --client-key=user.key --embed-certs
```

As user, let's try to list the nodes and Pods with this userconfig file:

```
$ kubectl --kubeconfig=userconfig get nodes
NAME         STATUS    ROLES     AGE    VERSION
controller   Ready     master    8h     v1.18.6
worker-0     Ready     <none>    8h     v1.18.6
worker-1     Ready     <none>    8h     v1.18.6

$ kubectl --kubeconfig=userconfig get pods
Error from server (Forbidden): pods is forbidden: User "user"
cannot list resource "pods" in API group "" in the
namespace "default"
```

The user can see nodes as expected and, hopefully, does not have the right to get Pods, as only explicit given accesses are authorized.

HTTP Basic Auth

For the Kubernetes API server to support HTTP Basic Authentication, you must specify the following option:

```
--basic-auth-file=somefile
```

Let's create the /etc/kubernetes/pki/basic-auth file with this content:

```
$ echo mypassword,pmartin,pmartin | \
  sudo tee /etc/kubernetes/pki/basic-auth
$ sudo chmod 600 /etc/kubernetes/pki/basic-auth
```

And add the option to the /etc/kubernetes/manifests/kube-apiserver.yaml file:

```
[...]
spec:
  containers:
  - command:
    - kube-apiserver
    - --advertise-address=10.240.0.10
    - --allow-privileged=true
    - --authorization-mode=Node,RBAC
    - --basic-auth-file=/etc/kubernetes/pki/basic-auth
[...]
```

Verify that the API server restarted to get the changes into account, by looking at the AGE information:

```
$ kubectl get pods -n kube-system kube-apiserver-controller
NAME                        READY   STATUS    RESTARTS   AGE
kube-apiserver-controller   1/1     Running   3          15s
```

Now that the user pmartin is registered in the API server, let's create a kubeconfig file for this user.

There are three parts in the kubeconfig file: server information, user information, and context information.

The command kubectl config set-cluster is used to write server information.

> Note in the following commands the presence of the
> flag --kubeconfig=userconfig. When the flag is set,
> the kubectl tool will work on this file, instead of on
> the default one ~/.kube/config:

```
$ CLUSTER_ENDPOINT=$(kubectl config view --minify --raw -o
jsonpath='{.clusters[0].cluster.server}')
$ CLUSTER_CA=$(kubectl config view --minify --raw -o
jsonpath='{.clusters[0].cluster.certificate-authority-data}')
$ echo -n $CLUSTER_CA | base64 -d > cluster.crt
$ CLUSTER_NAME=$(kubectl config view --minify --raw -o
jsonpath='{.clusters[0].name}')
$ kubectl --kubeconfig=userconfig config set-cluster $CLUSTER_
NAME \
    --server=$CLUSTER_ENDPOINT \
    --certificate-authority=cluster.crt --embed-certs
Cluster "cka" set.
```

The command kubectl config set-credentials is used to write user information:

```
$ USER_NAME=pmartin
$ kubectl --kubeconfig=userconfig config set-credentials $USER_
NAME \
    --username=pmartin --password=mypassword
User "pmartin" set.
```

The command kubectl config set-context is used to write context information and kubectl config use-context to select the current context:

```
$ kubectl --kubeconfig=userconfig config set-context default \
    --cluster=$CLUSTER_NAME \
    --user=$USER_NAME \
    --namespace=default
Context "default" created.
$ kubectl --kubeconfig=userconfig config use-context default
Switched to context "default".
```

The admin can authorize the user to read information about nodes with these commands (more on this in the section "Authorization"):

```
$ kubectl create clusterrole nodes-read \
    --verb=get,list,watch --resource=nodes
clusterrole.rbac.authorization.k8s.io/nodes-read created
$ kubectl create clusterrolebinding pmartin-nodes-read \
    --clusterrole=nodes-read --user=pmartin
clusterrolebinding.rbac.authorization.k8s.io/pmartin-nodes-read
created
```

The admin can now send this userconfig file to the user.

As pmartin, let's try to list the nodes and Pods with this userconfig file:

```
$ kubectl --kubeconfig=userconfig get nodes
NAME         STATUS   ROLES    AGE   VERSION
controller   Ready    master   8h    v1.18.6
worker-0     Ready    <none>   8h    v1.18.6
worker-1     Ready    <none>   8h    v1.18.6
```

```
$ kubectl --kubeconfig=userconfig get pods
Error from server (Forbidden): pods is forbidden: User
"pmartin" cannot list resource "pods" in API group "" in the
namespace "default"
```

The user can see nodes as expected and, hopefully, does not have the right to get Pods, as only explicit given accesses are authorized.

Bearer Token Authentication

For the Kubernetes API server to support Bearer Token Authentication, you must specify the following option:

```
--token-auth-file=somefile
```

Let's create the /etc/kubernetes/pki/tokens file with this content:

```
$ echo 22C1192A24CE822DDB2CB578BBBD8,foobar,foobar | \
  sudo tee /etc/kubernetes/pki/tokens
$ sudo chmod 600 /etc/kubernetes/pki/tokens
```

And add the option to the /etc/kubernetes/manifests/kube-apiserver.yaml file:

```
[...]
spec:
  containers:
  - command:
    - kube-apiserver
    - --advertise-address=10.240.0.10
    - --allow-privileged=true
    - --authorization-mode=Node,RBAC
    - --token-auth-file=/etc/kubernetes/pki/tokens
[...]
```

Verify that the API server restarted to get the changes into account, by looking at the AGE information:

```
$ kubectl get pods -n kube-system kube-apiserver-controller
NAME                         READY   STATUS    RESTARTS   AGE
kube-apiserver-controller    1/1     Running   3          15s
```

Now that the user foobar is registered in the API server, let's create a kubeconfig file for this user.

There are three parts in the kubeconfig file: server information, user information, and context information.

The command kubectl config set-cluster is used to write server information.

> Note in the following commands the presence of the
> flag --kubeconfig=userconfig. When the flag is set,
> the kubectl tool will work on this file, instead of on
> the default one ~/.kube/config:

```
$ CLUSTER_ENDPOINT=$(kubectl config view --minify --raw -o
jsonpath='{.clusters[0].cluster.server}')
$ CLUSTER_CA=$(kubectl config view --minify --raw -o
jsonpath='{.clusters[0].cluster.certificate-authority-data}')
$ echo -n $CLUSTER_CA | base64 -d > cluster.crt
$ CLUSTER_NAME=$(kubectl config view --minify --raw -o
jsonpath='{.clusters[0].name}')
$ kubectl --kubeconfig=userconfig config set-cluster $CLUSTER_
NAME \
   --server=$CLUSTER_ENDPOINT \
   --certificate-authority=cluster.crt --embed-certs
Cluster "cka" set.
```

The command kubectl config set-credentials is used to write user information:

```
$ USER_NAME=foobar
$ kubectl --kubeconfig=userconfig config set-credentials $USER_
NAME \
    --token=22C1192A24CE822DDB2CB578BBBD8
User "foobar" set.
```

The command kubectl config set-context is used to write context information and kubectl config use-context to select the current context:

```
$ kubectl --kubeconfig=userconfig config set-context default \
    --cluster=$CLUSTER_NAME \
    --user=$USER_NAME \
    --namespace=default
Context "default" created.
$ kubectl --kubeconfig=userconfig config use-context default
Switched to context "default".
```

The admin can authorize the user to read information about nodes with these commands (more on this in the section "Authorization"):

```
$ kubectl create clusterrole nodes-read \
    --verb=get,list,watch --resource=nodes
clusterrole.rbac.authorization.k8s.io/nodes-read created
$ kubectl create clusterrolebinding foobar-nodes-read \
    --clusterrole=nodes-read --user=foobar
clusterrolebinding.rbac.authorization.k8s.io/foobar-nodes-read
created
```

The admin can now send this userconfig file to the user.

As foobar, let's try to list the nodes and Pods with this userconfig file:

```
$ kubectl --kubeconfig=userconfig get nodes
NAME         STATUS    ROLES     AGE    VERSION
controller   Ready     master    8h     v1.18.6
worker-0     Ready     <none>    8h     v1.18.6
worker-1     Ready     <none>    8h     v1.18.6

$ kubectl --kubeconfig=userconfig get pods
Error from server (Forbidden): pods is forbidden: User "foobar"
cannot list resource\
"pods" in API group "" in the namespace "default"
```

The user can see nodes as expected and, hopefully, does not have the right to get Pods, as only explicit given accesses are authorized.

Service Account Authentication

In contrast to normal users, service accounts are managed by the Kubernetes API. The authentication is handled by JSON Web Tokens (JWTs).

When a ServiceAccount is created in a namespace, the *Token controller* creates a Secret in the same namespace, with a name prefixed by the service account name, and populates it with the public CA of the API server, a signed token, and the name of the current namespace.

When a namespace is created, the *Service Account controller* creates a default service account in this namespace. This creation in turn leads to the creation of the associated Secret.

A serviceAccountName field of the Pod spec indicates which service account is attached to the Pod. By default, if you do not specify any service account name, its value is default. You can set the automountServiceAccountToken field of the Pod spec to false to indicate that no service account should be used.

The Secret associated with the Pod's service account is automatically mounted into the Pod filesystem, in a well-known directory. The Kubernetes clients inside the Pod are aware of this path and use these credentials to connect to the API server.

As an example, let's create a service account and use it for a container containing the kubectl command, to test the accesses from inside the container:

```
# Create a service account for a kubectl pod
$ kubectl create serviceaccount kubectl
serviceaccount/kubectl created

# Get the name of the associated secret
$ SECRET_NAME=$(kubectl get sa kubectl -o jsonpath='{.
secrets[0].name}')

# Show the secret contents
$ kubectl get secret $SECRET_NAME -o yaml
[...]

# Create the nodes-read cluster role
$ kubectl create clusterrole nodes-read \
    --verb=get,list,watch --resource=nodes
clusterrole.rbac.authorization.k8s.io/nodes-read created

# Bind the nodes-read role to the service account kubectl in
default namespace
$ kubectl create clusterrolebinding default-kubectl-nodes-read
    --clusterrole=nodes-read --serviceaccount=default:kubectl
clusterrolebinding.rbac.authorization.k8s.io/default-kubectl-
nodes-read created
```

```
# Execute kubectl container with kubectl service account
$ kubectl run kubectl \
   --image=bitnami/kubectl:latest \
   --serviceaccount=kubectl \
   --command sh -- -c "sleep $((10**10))"
pod/kubectl created

# Connect into the kubectl container
$ kubectl exec -it kubectl bash

# Get nodes
$ kubectl get nodes
NAME          STATUS    ROLES     AGE    VERSION
controller    Ready     master    10h    v1.18.6
worker-0      Ready     <none>    10h    v1.18.6
worker-1      Ready     <none>    10h    v1.18.6

# Try to get pods
$ kubectl get pods
Error from server (Forbidden): pods is forbidden: User "system:
serviceaccount:default:kubectl" cannot list resource "pods"
in API group "" in the namespace "default"

# Show the mounted files from service account secret
$ ls /var/run/secrets/kubernetes.io/serviceaccount/
ca.crt namespace token
```

Service Account Outside the Cluster

Note that the token associated with a service account is also usable
from outside the cluster. You can, for example, create a kubeconfig file
containing this token and use it from your dev machine:

```
$ CLUSTER_ENDPOINT=$(kubectl config view --minify --raw -o
jsonpath='{.clusters[0].cluster.server}')
```

```
$ CLUSTER_CA=$(kubectl config view --minify --raw -o
jsonpath='{.clusters[0].cluster.certificate-authority-data}')
$ echo -n $CLUSTER_CA | base64 -d > cluster.crt
$ CLUSTER_NAME=$(kubectl config view --minify --raw -o
jsonpath='{.clusters[0].name}')

$ kubectl --kubeconfig=saconfig config set-cluster $CLUSTER_
NAME \
   --server=$CLUSTER_ENDPOINT \
   --certificate-authority=cluster.crt --embed-certs
Cluster "cka" set.

$ USER_NAME=kubectl
$ SECRET_NAME=$(kubectl get sa kubectl -o jsonpath='{.
secrets[0].name}')
$ TOKEN=$(kubectl get secrets $SECRET_NAME -o jsonpath='{.data.
token}' | base64 -d)
$ kubectl --kubeconfig=saconfig config set-credentials $USER_
NAME \
   --token=$TOKEN
User "kubectl" set.

$ kubectl --kubeconfig=saconfig config set-context default \
   --cluster=$CLUSTER_NAME \
   --user=$USER_NAME \
   --namespace=default
Context "default" created.
$ kubectl --kubeconfig=saconfig config use-context default
Switched to context "default".
```

```
# List the nodes
$ kubectl --kubeconfig=saconfig get nodes
NAME         STATUS    ROLES     AGE    VERSION
controller   Ready     master    10h    v1.18.6
worker-0     Ready     <none>    10h    v1.18.6
worker-1     Ready     <none>    10h    v1.18.6

# Try to list the pods
$ kubectl --kubeconfig=saconfig get pods
Error from server (Forbidden): pods is forbidden: User
"system:serviceaccount:default:kubectl" cannot list resource
"pods" in API group "" in the namespace "default"
```

Authorization

The Kubernetes API is a REST API. The authorization for an operation is evaluated at the request level. The user has to be granted access to all parts of the request against all policies to be authorized for this request. Admission controllers can be used to fine-tune the parts of a request authorized for a user.

Authorization is managed by modules, and several modules can be installed at the same time. Each module is checked in sequence, and the first allowing or denying the request stops the process of authorization. If no module has an opinion on the request, then the request is denied.

The following modules are available:

- ABAC: Attribute-based access control

- RBAC: Role-based access control

- Webhook: HTTP callback mode

- Node: Special-purpose module for kubelets

- AlwaysDeny: Blocks all requests, for testing purpose

- AlwaysAllow: To completely disable authorization

To select the modules to use, you have to specify their names in the `--authorization-mode` flag of the `apiserver` service. For a cluster installed with kubeadm, the default value of the flag is `--authorization-mode=Node,RBAC`.

Anatomy of an API Server Request

Resource Requests

Resource requests are used to operate on Kubernetes resources. The endpoints of resource requests are of the form

- `/api/v1/...` for the resources of the core group

- `/apis/<group>/<version>/...` for resources of other APIs

Endpoints for **namespaced resources** are of the form

- `/api/v1/namespaces/<namespace>/<resource>`

- `/apis/<group>/<version>/namespaces/<namespace>/<resource>`

Endpoints for n**on-namespaced resources** are of the form

- `/api/v1/<resource>`

- `/apis/<group>/<version>/<resource>`

For resource requests, an **API request verb** is used. Common verbs are

- `create` to create a new resource object

- `update` to replace a resource object with a new one

- `patch` to change specific fields of a resource object

- get to retrieve a resource object

- list to retrieve all resource objects within one namespace or across all namespaces

- watch to stream events (create, update, delete) on object(s)

- delete to delete a resource object

- deletecollection to delete all resource objects within one namespace

You can obtain the list of all the resources with their API group and their supported verbs and whether they are namespaced or not with the command kubectl api-resources -o wide.

Non-resource Requests

Non-resource requests are all the other requests and used to access information about the cluster.

For non-resource requests, an **HTTP request verb** is used, corresponding to lowercased HTTP methods, like get, post, put, and delete.

Request Attributes for Authorization

The attributes taken into account for authorization are

- Attributes from authentication:

  - user: The authenticated user

  - group: List of group names to which the user belongs

  - extra: Key-value pairs provided by the authentication layer

- Attributes from request:
  - For a resource request:
    - API group (empty for *core* group)
    - Namespace (for namespaced resource requests only)
    - Resource
    - Resource name (mandatory for get, update, patch, and delete verbs)
    - Subresource name (optional)
    - API request verb
  - For a non-resource request:
    - Request path
    - HTTP request verb

RBAC Mode

The RBAC mode introduces two concepts: the **Role**, which defines a list of permissions, and the **role binding**, which binds a Role to a user or a group of users (normal users, groups, or service accounts).

Role and ClusterRole

Two resources are defined, depending on whether the role is defined within a namespace with Role or cluster-wide with ClusterRole.

The Role and ClusterRole specs contain a rules field, an array of PolicyRule structures containing these subfields:

- `verbs`: List of allowed verbs, or `VerbAll` (or "*" in YAML) to bypass verification on this field

- `apiGroups`: List of allowed API groups, or `APIGroupAll` (or "*" in YAML) to bypass verification on this field

- `resources`: List of allowed resources, or `ResourceAll` (or "*" in YAML) to bypass verification on this field

- `resourceNames`: List of allowed objects, or empty to bypass verification on this field

- `nonResourceURLs`: List of allowed non-resource URLs (for ClusterRole only), or empty to bypass verification on this field

Each PolicyRule represents a set of permissions to grant for this role.

For a request to be allowed for a role, the verb, API group, resource, resource name, and non-resource URL attributes (if applicable) of the request must be present in the corresponding field in any policy rule of the role when the verification is active for this field.

A role is used to grant access to namespaced resources in the namespace the role is defined.

A cluster role is used to grant access to

- Namespaced resources (like pods) in any namespace

- Namespaced resources (like pods) across all namespaces (using the –all-namespaces flag)

- Non-namespaced resources (like nodes)

- Non-resource endpoints (like `/healthz`)

RoleBinding and ClusterRoleBinding

RoleBinding and ClusterRoleBinding specs both contain a roleRef field (a RoleRef structure) and a subjects field (an array of Subject structures).

These role bindings grant the referenced role to the specified subjects. The roleRef field references

- For a ClusterRoleBinding, a ClusterRole

- For a RoleBinding, a ClusterRole or a Role in the same namespace

The RoleRef structure is composed of the fields

- apiGroup: Must be rbac.authorization.k8s.io

- kind: Must be Role or ClusterRole

- name: The name of Role or ClusterRole

The Subject structure is composed of the fields

- apiGroup: "" for ServiceAccount, rbac.authorization.k8s.io for User and Group

- kind: Must be User, Group, or ServiceAccount

- name: Name of the User/Group/ServiceAccount subject

- namespace: Namespace of the subject, for ServiceAccount

The different possible bindings are

- A RoleBinding referencing a Role: Gives access to namespaced resources in the namespace of the role and role binding

- A RoleBinding referencing a ClusterRole: Gives access to namespaced resources in the namespace of the role binding (used to reuse a ClusterRole in different namespaces with different subjects)

- A ClusterRoleBinding referencing a ClusterRole: Gives access to namespaced resources in all namespaces and across all namespaces, to non-namespaced resources, and to non-resource endpoints

Examples

Here are some examples of Role definitions and their significations.

The role-read role allows the user to get and list all namespaced resources in the default namespace:

```
apiVersion: rbac.authorization.k8s.io/v1
kind: Role
metadata:
  name: role-read
  namespace: default
rules:
- apiGroups:
  - "*"
  resources:
  - "*"
  verbs:
  - "get"
  - "list"

---
```

```
apiVersion: rbac.authorization.k8s.io/v1
kind: RoleBinding
metadata:
  name: role-read
  namespace: default
roleRef:
  apiGroup: rbac.authorization.k8s.io
  kind: Role
  name: role-read
subjects:
- apiGroup: rbac.authorization.k8s.io
  kind: User
  name: user
```

You can also create these resources in imperative mode:

```
$ kubectl create role role-read --verb=get,
list --resource="*.*"
role.rbac.authorization.k8s.io/role-read created
$ kubectl create rolebinding role-read --role=role-
read --user=user
rolebinding.rbac.authorization.k8s.io/role-read created
```

These requests will be authorized:

```
$ export KUBECONFIG=userconfig
$ kubectl get pods kubectl # get core/pods
$ kubectl get pods # list core/pods
$ kubectl get deployments # list extensions/deployments
```

These requests will not be authorized:

```
$ export KUBECONFIG=userconfig
$ kubectl get namespaces # namespaces are cluster-scope
```

```
$ kubectl delete pods kubectl # delete not in verbs
$ kubectl get pods -n kube-system # not in default namespace
```

You can now delete the role and role binding:

```
$ unset KUBECONFIG
$ kubectl delete rolebinding role-read
rolebinding.rbac.authorization.k8s.io "role-read" deleted
$ kubectl delete role role-read
role.rbac.authorization.k8s.io "role-read" deleted
```

The role-create-pod role allows the user to create Pods in the default namespace:

```
apiVersion: rbac.authorization.k8s.io/v1
kind: Role
metadata:
  name: role-create-pod
rules:
- apiGroups:
  - ""
  resources:
  - "pods"
  verbs:
  - "create"

---

apiVersion: rbac.authorization.k8s.io/v1
kind: RoleBinding
metadata:
  name: role-create-pod
roleRef:
```

```
  apiGroup: rbac.authorization.k8s.io
  kind: Role
  name: role-create-pod
subjects:
- apiGroup: rbac.authorization.k8s.io
  kind: User
  name: user
```

You can also create these resources in imperative mode:

```
$ kubectl create role role-create-pod --resource=
pods --verb=create
role.rbac.authorization.k8s.io/role-create-pod created
$ kubectl create rolebinding role-create-pod --role=role-
create-pod --user=user
rolebinding.rbac.authorization.k8s.io/role-create-pod created
```

This request will be authorized:

```
$ export KUBECONFIG=userconfig
$ kubectl run nginx --image=nginx # create core/pods
```

These requests will not be authorized:

```
$ export KUBECONFIG=userconfig
$ kubectl get pods # list verb
$ kubectl get pods nginx # get verb
$ kubectl create deployment nginx --image=nginx # extensions/
deployments
$ kubectl run nginx --image=nginx -n other # other namespace
```

You can now delete the role and role binding:

```
$ unset KUBECONFIG
$ kubectl delete rolebinding role-create-pod
rolebinding.rbac.authorization.k8s.io "role-create-pod" deleted
```

```
$ kubectl delete role role-create-pod
role.rbac.authorization.k8s.io "role-create-pod" deleted
```

The `cluster-role-read` role allows the user to get and list all namespaced resources in and across all namespaces, as well as all non-namespaced resources:

```
apiVersion: rbac.authorization.k8s.io/v1
kind:ClusterRole
metadata:
  name: cluster-role-read
rules:
- apiGroups:
  - "*"
  resources:
  - "*"
  verbs:
  - "get"
  - "list"

---

apiVersion: rbac.authorization.k8s.io/v1
kind: ClusterRoleBinding
metadata:
  name: cluster-role-read
roleRef:
  apiGroup: rbac.authorization.k8s.io
  kind:ClusterRole
  name: cluster-role-read
subjects:
- apiGroup: rbac.authorization.k8s.io
  kind: User
  name: user
```

You can also create these resources in imperative mode:

```
$ kubectl create clusterrole cluster-role-read --resource=
"*.*" --verb=get,list
clusterrole.rbac.authorization.k8s.io/cluster-role-read created
$ kubectl create clusterrolebinding cluster-role-
read --clusterrole=cluster-role-rea\
d --user=user
clusterrolebinding.rbac.authorization.k8s.io/cluster-role-read
created
```

These requests will be authorized:

```
$ export KUBECONFIG=userconfig
$ kubectl get pods kubectl # get core/pods
$ kubectl get pods # list core/pods
$ kubectl get pods -n kube-system # list core/pods in other
  namespace
$ kubectl get pods -A # list core/pods across all namespaces
$ kubectl get deployments # list extensions/deployments
$ kubectl get nodes # list (non-namespaced) nodes
```

These requests will not be authorized:

```
$ export KUBECONFIG=userconfig
$ kubectl delete pods kubectl # delete not in verbs
```

You can now delete the role and role binding:

```
$ unset KUBECONFIG
$ kubectl delete rolebinding cluster-role-read
rolebinding.rbac.authorization.k8s.io "cluster-role-read"
deleted
$ kubectl delete role cluster-role-read
role.rbac.authorization.k8s.io "cluster-role-read" deleted
```

Security Contexts

You can configure security contexts at Pod and container levels.

At Pod Level

The Pod spec defines several fields in its `PodSecurityContext` structure, accessible in the `securityContext` field.

User and Groups

By default, the processes inside the containers of a Pod run with the `root` rights. Thanks to the container isolation, the `root` rights inside the container are limited.

But in some circumstances, for example, when mounting external filesystems inside the container, you would like that the processes run with specific user and group rights.

The `runAsNonRoot` field helps to ensure that the processes in containers of the Pod are running as non-root user. If no user is defined in the container image definition and if no `runAsUSer` is defined here or in the `SecurityContext` at container level, kubelet will refuse to start the Pod.

With the `runAsUser`, `runAsGroup`, and `supplementalGroups` fields, you can affect the first process of the containers of the Pod to a specific user and a specific group and add these processes to supplemental groups.

As an example, when running a Pod with the following specs:

```
apiVersion: apps/v1
kind: Deployment
metadata:
  labels:
    app: box
  name: box
```

```
spec:
  selector:
    matchLabels:
      app: box
  template:
    metadata:
      labels:
        app: box
    spec:
      securityContext:
        runAsNonRoot: true
        runAsUser: 1000
        runAsGroup: 1001
        supplementalGroups:
        - 1002
        - 1003
      containers:
      - image: busybox
        name: box
        command:
        - sh
        - c
        - "touch  /tmp/ready  &&   sleep  $((10**10))"
```

you can examine the users and groups for processes and created files:

```
$ ps -o pid,user,group,comm
PID    USER      GROUP     COMMAND
    1  1000      1001      sleep
    7  1000      1001      sh
   14  1000      1001      ps
```

```
$  ls -l /tmp/ready
-rw-r--r--  1 1000  1001  0 Jan 23 09:52 /tmp/ready
$ id
uid=1000 gid=1001 groups=1002,1003
```

SELinux Options

seLinuxOptions applies a SELinux context to all containers of the Pod.

Sysctls

If you want to set kernel parameters from inside a container, you will get the following error:

```
$ sysctl -w kernel.shm_rmid_forced=1
sysctl: error setting key 'kernel.shm_rmid_forced': Read-only
file system
```

You can pass these values from the Pod spec:

```
apiVersion: apps/v1
kind: Deployment
metadata:
  labels:
    app: box
  name: box
spec:
  selector:
    matchLabels:
      app: box
  template:
    metadata:
      labels:
        app: box
```

```
spec:
  securityContext:
    sysctls:
    - name: kernel.shm_rmid_forced
      value: "1"
  containers:
  - image: busybox
    name: box
```

Note that only *safe* sysctls are allowed to be changed by default. If you want to change other sysctls, you will need to allow them via the *kubelet* configuration (using `kubelet --allowed-unsafe-sysctls 'comma-separated list of sysctls'`).

At Container Level

The Container spec defines several fields in its `SecurityContext` structure, accessible in the `securityContext` field.

User and Groups

As within the Pod spec, you can assert that the image is running as non-root user with the `runAsNonRoot` field, and you can specify a specific user and group with `runAsGroup` and `runAsUser` for the first process of the container.

If specified at both Pod and container levels, the information in the Container spec is used.

SELinux Options

`seLinuxOptions` applies a SELinux context to this container. If specified at both Pod and container levels, the information in the Container spec is used.

Capabilities

- `capabilities`

  Modifies initial capabilities for the container initial process

- `allowPrivilegeEscalation`

  Indicates if the processes can get more capabilities at runtime

Others

- `privileged`

  This is equivalent as running as root in the host. **Don't do this unless you exactly know what you are doing**.

- `readOnlyRootFilesystem`

  The processes won't be able to change or create files into the container filesystem. This prevents attackers from installing new programs in the container, for example.

Network Policies

By default, traffic between Pods of a cluster is unrestricted. You can fine-tune the traffic authorization between the Pods by declaring network policies, using the `NetworkPolicy` resource.

The spec of the `NetworkPolicy` resource contains the fields

- `podSelector`: Selects Pods to which this policy applies. An empty value matches all Pods in the namespace.

- `policyTypes`: Indicates if you want to apply `Ingress` rules, `Egress` rules, or both.

- ingress: The allowed Ingress rules for the selected
  Pods.

- egress: The allowed Egress rules for the selected Pods.

First, create three Pods (an Apache server, an nginx server, and a
busybox Pod) and two Services to expose the two web servers:

```
apiVersion: apps/v1
kind: Deployment
metadata:
  name: box-deployment
spec:
  selector:
    matchLabels:
      app: box
  template:
    metadata:
      labels:
        app: box
    spec:
      containers:
      - name: box
        image: busybox
        command:
        - sh
        - c
        - "sleep $((10**10))"

---

apiVersion: apps/v1
kind: Deployment
metadata:
  name: httpd-deployment
```

```
spec:
  selector:
    matchLabels:
      app: httpd
  template:
    metadata:
      labels:
        app: httpd
      spec:
        containers:
        - name: httpd
          image: httpd

---

apiVersion: apps/v1
kind: Deployment
metadata:
  name: nginx-deployment
spec:
  selector:
    matchLabels:
      app: nginx
  template:
    metadata:
      labels:
        app: nginx
      spec:
        containers:
        - name: nginx
          image: nginx

---
```

```
apiVersion: v1
kind:  Service
metadata:
  name: httpd-service
spec:
  type: ClusterIP
  selector:
    app: httpd
  ports:
  - port: 80

---

apiVersion: v1
kind:  Service
metadata:
  name: nginx-service
spec:
  type: ClusterIP
  selector:
    app: nginx
  ports:
  - port: 80
```

You can see that from the box container, you can access both apache and nginx:

```
$ kubectl exec -it box-deployment-xxxxxxxxxx-yyyyy sh
# wget -q http://httpd-service -O -
[... apache response ...]
# wget -q http://nginx-service -O -
[... nginx response ...]
```

With a first NetworkPolicy, you can disallow all Ingress traffic to the Pods:

```
apiVersion: networking.k8s.io/v1
kind: NetworkPolicy
metadata:
  name: netpol
spec:
  podSelector: {}
  policyTypes:
  - Ingress
```

You can see you cannot connect anymore to apache and nginx Pods from the box Pod:

```
$ kubectl exec -it box-deployment-xxxxxxxxxx-yyyyy sh
# wget -q http://httpd-service -O -
<no reply>
# wget -q http://nginx-service -O -
<no reply>
```

You can now allow traffic to port 80 of nginx from the box Pods:

```
apiVersion: networking.k8s.io/v1
kind: NetworkPolicy
metadata:
  name: netpol2
spec:
  podSelector:
    matchLabels:
      app: nginx
  policyTypes:
    - Ingress
```

```
  ingress:
  - ports:
    - port: 80
    from:
    - podSelector:
        matchLabels:
          app: box
```

Working with Private Docker Registries

Up to now, you have referenced public images to deploy containers. But when you will want to deploy your own applications, it is possible that you do not want to make your container images public, but store them in a private registry.

In this case, kubelet will need to get the necessary credentials to be able to download the images stored in the private registry.

Using imagePullSecrets

This is the recommended way to give access to the registry when you do not have access to the nodes or when nodes are created automatically.

The first step is to create a Secret containing the registry credentials.

If you already have logged in or can log in to the registry from your computer with the command docker login, you should have a file ~/. docker/config.json. You can then create a Secret from this file with the command

```
$ kubectl create secret generic regcred \
    --from-file=.dockerconfigjson=<path/to/.docker/config.json> \
    --type=kubernetes.io/dockerconfigjson
```

Or you can create a Secret from the login information:

```
$ kubectl create secret docker-registry regcred \
    --docker-server=$DOCKER_REGISTRY_SERVER \
    --docker-username=$DOCKER_USER \
    --docker-password=$DOCKER_PASSWORD \
    --docker-email=$DOCKER_EMAIL
```

Once the Secret is created in the namespace, you can reference it from Pod specs with the imagePullSecrets field (note that you could reference several Secrets, if your Pod contains several containers, getting images from different registries):

```
# box.yaml
apiVersion: apps/v1
kind: Deployment
metadata:
  labels:
    app: box
  name: box
spec:
  selector:
    matchLabels:
      app: box
  template:
    metadata:
      labels:
        app: box
    spec:
      imagePullSecrets:
      - name: regcred
      containers:
      - image: yourlogin/test
        name: box
```

153

An important thing to know is that once the image is downloaded by a node, all Pods executing on this same node will be allowed to use this image, even if they do not specify an imagePullSecrets.

To test it, first deploy the following Pod on a multi-worker cluster, and see on which node it is deployed:

```
$ kubectl apply -f box.yaml
deployment.apps/box created
$ kubectl get pods -o wide
NAME                    READY    STATUS    [...]    NODE
box-865486655c-c76sj    1/1      Running   [...]    worker-0
```

In this case, the image has been downloaded by worker-0. Now update the Deployment to remove the imagePullSecrets and deploy several replicas, so they will be deployed on other nodes too. Also set the imagePullPolicy to IfNotPresent, so kubelet will use an already present image if available:

```
$ kubectl delete -f box.yaml
deployment.apps "box" deleted
$ kubectl apply -f - <<EOF
apiVersion: apps/v1
kind: Deployment
metadata:
  labels:
    app: box
  name: box
spec:
  replicas: 2
  selector:
    matchLabels:
      app: box
```

```
  template:
    metadata:
      labels:
        app: box
    spec:
      containers:
      - image: yourlogin/test
        name: box
        imagePullPolicy: IfNotPresent
EOF
deployment.apps/box created
$ kubectl get pods -o wide
NAME                     READY   STATUS         AGE   [...]   NODE
box-865486655c-n4pg6     0/1     ErrImagePull   5s    [...]   worker-1
box-865486655c-w55kp     1/1     Running        5s    [...]   worker-0
```

You can see that the Pod in worker-0 started successfully, but the one in the other worker failed to get the image.

Pre-pulling Images on Nodes

You have seen it is only necessary that an image is pulled on the node to be available for Pods. So let's connect to the worker-1 node, connect to the Docker registry, and then manually pull the image:

```
$ gcloud compute ssh worker-1
Welcome to worker-1
$ sudo docker login
Username: yourlogin
Password:
$ docker pull yourlogin/test
docker.io/yourlogin/test:latest
```

If you go back to your computer, you can see that the Pod in `worker-1` can now be started:

```
$ kubectl get pods -o wide
NAME                      READY    STATUS    [...]    NODE
box-865486655c-2t6fw      1/1      Running   [...]    worker-1
box-865486655c-nnpr2      1/1      Running   [...]    worker-0
```

Giving Credentials to kubelet

In the previous step, you logged in the private registry to manually download the image. During login, Docker created a ~/.docker/config. json to store the credentials used during login.

You can copy this file in a directory recognized by kubelet, so kubelet will try to download images using these credentials:

```
$ gcloud compute ssh worker-1
Welcome to worker-1
$ cp $HOME/.docker/config.json /var/lib/kubelet/
$ sudo systemctl kubelet restart
```

## CHAPTER 12

Persistent Volumes

A persistent volume (**PV**) is a storage resource provisioned by the cluster administrators. The provisioning can be manual or automatic.

A PV declaration is made of two parts:

- Its capabilities (access modes, capacity, storage class, volume mode – filesystem or raw)

- Its implementation (local, NFS, cloud storage resource, etc.)

These storage resources are intended to be used by Pods, through the use of `PersistentVolumeClaims`: a Pod will claim a persistent volume with specific capabilities, and Kubernetes will try to find a persistent volume matching these capabilities (independently of the implementation details).

If available, the persistent volume will be mounted into the filesystem of the node deploying the Pod and finally exposed to the Pod. The implementation part indicates to kubelet how to mount the storage into a filesystem.

Creating an NFS Persistent Volume

As an example, we will manually create a PV implemented by an NFS volume.

© Philippe Martin 2021

P. Martin, *Kubernetes*, https://doi.org/10.1007/978-1-4842-6494-2_12

First, create an NFS volume in Google Cloud:

```
$ gcloud filestore instances create nfs-server \
    --project=$(gcloud config get-value project) \
    --zone=$(gcloud config get-value compute/zone) \
    --tier=STANDARD \
    --file-share=name="vol1",capacity=1TB \
    --network=name="kubernetes-cluster"
Waiting for [operation-...] to finish...done.
$ gcloud filestore instances describe nfs-server \
    --project=$(gcloud config get-value project) \
    --zone=$(gcloud config get-value compute/zone)
createTime: '2020-01-24T07:43:58.279881289Z'
fileShares:
- capacityGb: '1024'
  name: vol1
name: projects/yourproject/locations/us-west1-c/instances/nfs-
server
networks:
- ipAddresses:
  - 172.25.52.106 # Note this IP address
  network: kubernetes-cluster
  reservedIpRange: 172.25.52.104/29
state: READY
tier: STANDARD
```

On the workers, install the NFS drivers to be able to mount NFS filesystems:

Repeat these steps for each worker:

```
$ gcloud compute ssh worker-0
Welcome to worker-0
$ sudo apt-get -y update
$ sudo apt-get -y install nfs-common
```

You can test that the worker can mount the filesystem:

```
$ gcloud compute ssh worker-0
Welcome to worker-0
$ sudo mkdir /mnt/nfs
$ sudo mount 172.25.52.106:/vol1 /mnt/nfs
$ ls /mnt/nfs
lost+found
$ sudo umount /mnt/nfs
```

You can now define the NFS persistent volume:

```
apiVersion: v1
kind: PersistentVolume
metadata:
  name: pv-nfs
spec:
  # capabilities
  accessModes:
  - ReadWriteOnce
  - ReadOnlyMany
  - ReadWriteMany
  capacity:
    storage: 1Ti
  volumeMode: Filesystem
  # implementation
    nfs:
      path: /vol1
      server: 172.25.52.106
```

Access Modes

In a general way, a storage system can be accessed for read and write operations, and can or cannot be accessed by several clients for each of these operations simultaneously, depending on the technology used by the storage system.

The PersistentVolume accessModes field indicates what the capabilities of the underlying storage system are in terms of simultaneous access on read-only or read/write mode. Three values are defined:

ReadWriteOnce (RWO)

The storage is accessible for read and write operations by a single client.

ReadOnlyMany (ROX)

The storage is accessible for read-only operations, by several clients.

ReadWriteMany (RWX)

The storage is accessible for read and write operations, by several clients.

If the PV has a **Many** capability, several Pods will be able to use this PV at the same time. Note that for a PV to be used by several Pods, the access mode claimed must be the same by all the Pods; it is not possible that one Pod uses a ReadOnlyMany mode and another Pod uses ReadWriteMany on the same PV.

Claiming a Persistent Volume

When a Pod needs a persistent volume, it must **claim** one. It does not claim a particular persistent volume, but rather claims a list of capabilities. The persistent volume controller will affect the best possible persistent volume depending on the capabilities matching.

The PersistentVolumeClaim resource is used, and its Spec structure defines these fields:

accessModes

The access mode requested (see "Access modes").

selector

A label selector to match specific persistent volumes based on labels.

resources

The persistent volume must provide at least resources.requests.storage and, if defined, at most resources.limits.storage.

storageClassName

The storage provider can define different storage class names; you can specify which class the persistent volume should belong to.

volumeMode

The mode of storage: **filesystem** or **block**.

To continue the preceding example, you can create a claim that will match the provisioned NFS persistent volume – precisely, a volume accessible by several clients in read-write mode, with at least 500 Gi and at most 1.5 Ti of storage:

```
apiVersion: v1
kind: PersistentVolumeClaim
metadata:
  name: pv-rwx-500g
spec:
  storageClassName: ""
```

```
accessModes:
  - ReadWriteMany
resources:
  requests:
    storage: 500Gi
  limits:
    storage: 1500Gi
```

Now, you can deploy two Pods, using the same storage, one database system, and one box:

```
apiVersion: apps/v1
kind: StatefulSet
metadata:
  labels:
    app: pg
  name: pg
spec:
  serviceName: pg
  selector:
    matchLabels:
      app: pg
  template:
    metadata:
      labels:
        app: pg
    spec:
      containers:
      - image: postgres
        name: pg
        env:
        - name: PGDATA
```

```
          value: /var/lib/postgresql/data/db-files
        volumeMounts:
        - name: data
          mountPath: /var/lib/postgresql/data
      volumes:
      - name: data
        persistentVolumeClaim:
          claimName: pv-rwx-500g
          readOnly: false

---

apiVersion: apps/v1
kind: StatefulSet
metadata:
  labels:
    app: box
  name: box
spec:
  serviceName: box
  selector:
    matchLabels:
      app: box
  template:
    metadata:
      labels:
        app: box
    spec:
      containers:
      - image: busybox
        name: box
        volumeMounts:
```

```
    - name: data
      mountPath: /mnt
    command:
      - sh
      - -c
      - "sleep $((10**10))"
    volumes:
    - name: data
      persistentVolumeClaim:
        claimName: pv-rwx-500g
        readOnly: false
```

If you examine the logs of the database Pod, using the command kubectl logs db-0, you can see that the system created a new database and stores its files on the directory:

`/var/lib/postgresql/data/db-files`

From the box Pod, you can access the same filesystem:

```
$ kubectl exec -it box-0 sh
# ls /mnt/db-files/
PG_VERSION              pg_multixact            pg_tblspc
base                    pg_notify               pg_twophase
global                  pg_replslot             pg_wal
pg_commit_ts            pg_serial               pg_xact
pg_dynshmem             pg_snapshots            postgresql.auto.conf
pg_hba.conf             pg_stat                 postgresql.conf
pg_ident.conf           pg_stat_tmp             postmaster.opts
pg_logical              pg_subtrans             postmaster.pid
```

Cleanup

Persistent volumes are expensive. Remember to delete the NFS volume when you do not need it anymore:

```
$ gcloud filestore instances delete nfs-server \
    --project=$(gcloud config get-value project) \
    --zone=$(gcloud config get-value compute/zone)
```

Using Auto-provisioned Persistent Volumes

Generally, Kubernetes engines in the cloud provide auto-provisioned persistent volumes. For example, in Google Cloud GKE, GCE persistent disks are used for auto-provisioned persistent volumes.

First, deploy a Kubernetes cluster:

```
$ gcloud beta container clusters create "kluster" \
    --project $(gcloud config get-value project) \
    --zone $(gcloud config get-value compute/zone) \
    --cluster-version "1.15.12-gke.2" \
    --machine-type "g1-small" \
    --image-type "COS" \
    --disk-type "pd-standard" \
    --disk-size "30" \
    --num-nodes "1"
[...]
$ gcloud container clusters get-credentials kluster \
    --zone $(gcloud config get-value compute/zone) \
    --project $(gcloud config get-value project)
```

Now create a PVC:

```
# auto-pvc.yaml
apiVersion: v1
kind: PersistentVolumeClaim
metadata:
  name: disk-rwo-10g
spec:
  accessModes:
    - ReadWriteOnce
  resources:
    requests:
      storage: 10Gi
```

```
$ kubectl apply -f auto-pvc.yaml
persistentvolumeclaim/disk-rwo-10g created
$ kubectl get pvc
NAME    STATUS    VOLUME    CAPACITY    ACCESS MODES    STORAGECLASS    AGE
disk-rwo-10g    Bound    pvc-[...]    10Gi    RWO    standard    3s
$ kubectl get pv
NAME    CAPACITY    ACCESS MODES    RECLAIM POLICY    STATUS    CLAIM    \
    STORAGECLASS    REASON    AGE
pvc-[...]    10Gi    RWO    Delete    Bound    default/disk-rwo-10g\
    standard            3s
```

You can see that as soon as you created a claim, a PV resource has been created.

You can now deploy a Pod using this claim:

```
apiVersion: apps/v1
kind: StatefulSet
metadata:
  labels:
```

```
    app: box
  name: box
spec:
  serviceName: box
  selector:
    matchLabels:
      app: box
  template:
    metadata:
      labels:
        app: box
    spec:
      containers:
      - image: busybox
        name: box
        volumeMounts:
        - name: data
          mountPath: /mnt
        command:
          - sh
          - -c
          - "sleep $((10**10))"
      volumes:
      - name: data
        persistentVolumeClaim:
          claimName: disk-rwo-10g
          readOnly: false
```

When you do not need the persistent volume anymore, you can release it by deleting the claim:

```
$ kubectl delete pvc disk-rwo-10g
persistentvolumeclaim "disk-rwo-10g" deleted
$ kubectl get pv
No resources found in default namespace.
```

Cleanup

Remove the previously deployed Kubernetes cluster:

```
$ gcloud beta container clusters delete "kluster" \
    --project $(gcloud config get-value project) \
    --zone $(gcloud config get-value compute/zone)
```

CHAPTER 13

Multi-container Pod Design Patterns

A Pod is the minimal piece deployable in a Kubernetes cluster. A Pod can contain one or several containers.

When a Pod contains several containers, the containers share network and storage resources.

A single Pod having several containers has to be used with care. You should use this pattern only when the containers are tightly coupled and when one container is the principal one and the others are helping the first one.

The Kubernetes community has described these following design patterns using multi-container Pods.

Init Container

The *Init container pattern* can be used when you want to initialize some resources before the main container runs or wait for a specific external state.

The spec of the Pod resource contains an `initContainers` field. This field contains an array of container definitions.

Init containers defined through this field are run in a sequence and in the order of appearance, before the main containers. If an init container fails, the Pod immediately fails.

© Philippe Martin 2021
P. Martin, *Kubernetes*, https://doi.org/10.1007/978-1-4842-6494-2_13

Initialize a Storage

In this first example, an Init container loads files from a Google Cloud Bucket and stores these files in a volatile volume. The main container, an nginx server, mounts the same volatile volume and serves these files:

```
apiVersion: apps/v1
kind: Deployment
metadata:
  name: website
spec:
  selector:
    matchLabels:
      app: website
  template:
    metadata:
      labels:
        app: website
    spec:
      volumes:
      - name: static-files
        emptyDir:
          sizeLimit: 20Mi
      initContainers:
      - name: copy-static-files
        image: gcr.io/cloud-builders/gcloud
        command:
        - "bash"
        - "-c"
        - "gsutil cp -R $(SOURCE)/* /mnt/"
        env:
        - name: SOURCE
```

```
      value: gs://my-gcp-project/my-bucket
    volumeMounts:
    - mountPath: /mnt
      name: static-files
      readOnly: false
  containers:
  - name: website
    image: nginx
    ports:
    - containerPort: 80
    volumeMounts:
    - mountPath: /usr/share/nginx/html
      name: static-files
      readOnly: true
```

Wait for Availability of Another Service

In this second example, an Init container tests if a backend service is available and terminates successfully when the service becomes available, so the main container can consider the backend is running at startup:

```
apiVersion: apps/v1
kind: Deployment
metadata:
  name: api
spec:
  selector:
    matchLabels:
      app: api
  template:
    metadata:
```

```
  labels:
    app: api
spec:
  initContainers:
  - name: wait-backend
    image: busybox
    args:
    - sh
    - -c
    - "until wget http://backend/; do sleep 1; done"
  containers:
  - name: api
    image: api
    ports:
    - containerPort: 80
```

Sidecar Container

A sidecar container is an additional container running in the same Pod as the main container, intended to assist the main container during its execution.

Its purpose is not defined by the design pattern; it can, for example, intercept the inbound traffic to adapt it before sending it to the main container, or it can intercept the outbound traffic to adapt it to the recipient, or it can aggregate logs created by the main container to expose them, just to name a few.

The following two design patterns, *adapter* and *ambassador*, are a specialization of the sidecar container pattern.

Adapter Container

An adapter container is a sidecar container, whose purpose is to intercept the inbound traffic to the Pod and adapt it to the protocol expected by the main container.

Using an adapter container, you can reuse a main container in different environments without changing its interfaces. The adapter container will be in charge of translating the protocol used by the caller to the protocol used by the main container.

Ambassador Container

An ambassador container is a sidecar container, whose purpose is to call an external service on behalf of the main container.

Using an ambassador container, you can reuse a main container in different environments, without the need to make it aware of all the protocols necessary to communicate with the external services, which could be of different nature depending on the environment.

As an example, consider the main container needs to access data from an external database. In the development environment, you want the data to be provided by an in-memory database, similar to SQLite. But in the production environment, the data must be provided by an external PostgreSQL database. Thanks to the ambassador container pattern, the main container would query to its ambassador container some set of data, and the ambassador would be specialized depending on the environment: the ambassador deployed in the development environment would query data from an SQLite database, while the ambassador deployed in the production environment would query data from a PostgreSQL database.

CHAPTER 14

Observability

When working with Kubernetes, observability is crucial. Kubernetes is made of an important quantity of moving parts, and you will need tools to understand what is happening or what happened between these different parts.

Debugging at the Kubernetes Level

First, you have to note that there are two types of Kubernetes resources: managed and unmanaged resources. A managed resource is recognizable because its definition contains a `spec` section and a `status` section. Controllers are responsible for managing such resources; they will read the `spec` section, will do their best to change the world to reflect these specifications, and then will report the state in the `status` section.

Other resources, like `ConfigMap`, `Secret`, `Volume`, `ServiceAccount`, `Role`, `RoleBinding`, and others, are unmanaged resources, and their purpose is to contain specific data used by other elements of the system.

The `kubectl describe` command is one of the first tools to use when you need to understand why your application does not work. Using this command, you can observe the state of your managed Kubernetes resources.

The output of this command generally starts with the metadata of the resource: name, namespace, labels, and annotations. The metadata are followed by a mix of the specifications and the status of the resource, in a human-readable way, usually in tabular form. At the end are displayed the events attached to this resource.

© Philippe Martin 2021
P. Martin, *Kubernetes*, https://doi.org/10.1007/978-1-4842-6494-2_14

An Event is a Kubernetes resource, used by the controllers and other Kubernetes elements, to log information. An event is of type *Normal* or *Warning*, indicates the time at which it happened, the action taken, the reason why the action was taken, which controller took the action and emitted the event, the resource the event is about, and a human-readable description of the event.

Reading these events, you will generally find the root cause of some problems in your cluster, including the following:

- A Pod is not schedulable, because the nodes do not have enough available resources.

- An image cannot be pulled.

- A volume, ConfigMap, or Secret is not available.

- A readiness or liveness probe of a container failed.

```
$ kubectl describe pods nginx-d9bc977d8-h66wf
Name:         nginx-d9bc977d8-h66wf
Namespace:    default
[...]
Events:
  Type    Reason     Age        From             Message
  ----    ------     ----       ----             -------
  Normal  Scheduled  <unknown>  default-scheduler Successfully
                                                  assigned
                                                  default/ngi\
nx-d9bc977d8-h66wf to worker-0
  Normal  Pulling    10s        kubelet, worker-0 Pulling
                                                  image
                                                  "nginx"
```

```
Normal  Pulled    9s        kubelet, worker-0 Successfully
                                               pulled image
                                               "nginx"
Normal  Created   9s        kubelet, worker-0 Created
                                               container
                                               nginx
Normal  Started   9s        kubelet, worker-0 Started
                                               container
                                               nginx
```

You can also observe all the events that are occurring in the cluster, with the command kubectl get events. You can add the -w option that will make the command wait for new events (you can terminate the command with Ctrl-C):

```
$ kubectl get events -w
LAST SEEN    TYPE      REASON             OBJECT
    MESSAGE
<unknown>    Normal    Scheduled          pod/nginx-d
    Successfully assigned default/nginx-d9bc977d8-h66wf to worker-0
4m20s        Normal    Pulling            pod/nginx-d
    Pulling image "nginx"
4m19s        Normal    Pulled             pod/nginx-d
    Successfully pulled image "nginx"
4m19s        Normal    Created            pod/nginx-d
    Created container nginx
4m19s        Normal    Started            pod/nginx-d
    Started container nginx
4m21s        Normal    Killing            pod/nginx-d
    Stopping container nginx
4m21s        Normal    SuccessfulCreate   rs/nginx-d
     Created pod: nginx-d9bc977d8-h66wf
```

Debugging Inside Containers

It is possible to execute commands from inside containers with the command kubectl exec. This implies that containers contain debug utilities.

Here's an example to list the files inside a given directory of the single container of an nginx Pod:

```
$ kubectl exec nginx-d9bc977d8-h66wf -- ls /usr/share/nginx/html
index.html
```

If you want to run an interactive command inside the container (a shell or another command interacting with the TTY), you will need to specify the --stdin and --tty flags (you can shorten them to -it):

```
$ kubectl exec -it nginx-d9bc977d8-h66wf -- bash
# ls /usr/share/nginx/html
index.html
[ other commands ]
# exit
```

Debugging Services

An important responsibility of Kubernetes is to expose Pods using Service and Ingress resources.

In this example, you will run two nginx replicas and make them available through a Service:

```
$ kubectl create deployment nginx --image=nginx
deployment.apps/nginx created
$ kubectl scale deployment/nginx --replicas=2
deployment.apps/nginx scaled
$ kubectl expose deployment nginx --port=80
service/nginx exposed
```

If everything goes well, the Service should expose the two Pods (in this case, requests to the Service are load-balanced between the two Pods). To be sure that the Service exposes two backends, you can examine the Endpoints resources:

```
$ kubectl get endpoints nginx
nginx    10.244.43.43:80,10.244.43.45:80 6s
```

The information is also available with the kubectl describe service command:

```
$ kubectl describe service nginx
Name:             nginx
Namespace:        default
Labels:           app=nginx
Annotations:      <none>
Selector:         app=nginx
Type:             ClusterIP
IP:               10.103.237.61
Port:             <unset> 80/TCP
TargetPort:       80/TCP
Endpoints:        10.244.43.43:80,10.244.43.45:80
Session Affinity: None
Events:           <none>
```

The commands show that the Service exposes two IP addresses. You can verify that these addresses match the addresses of the two nginx Pods with the command (note the -o wide option that will display more information, including the IP addresses of Pods)

```
$ kubectl get pods -l app=nginx -o wide
NAME                        READY   STATUS    RESTARTS   AGE
    IP    [...]
nginx-f89759699-b7lsq       1/1     Running   0          1m16s
    10.244.43.45 [...]
nginx-f89759699-l4f7c       1/1     Running   0          1m38s
    10.244.43.43 [...]
```

Logging

Containers have to output logs to standard output (stdout) or standard error (stderr) streams for the logs to be available within the Kubernetes infrastructure.

You can use the kubectl logs command to display the logs of a **particular pod**:

```
$ kubectl logs nginx
127.0.0.1 - - [01/Feb/2020:17:05:58 +0000] "GET / HTTP/1.1" 200
612 "-" "curl/7.58.0\
  " "-"
```

or a **set of Pods**, selected by their labels (use --prefix to differentiate the Pods):

```
$ kubectl logs -l app=nginx --prefix
[pod/nginx-86c57db685-cqm6c/nginx] 127.0.0.1 - - [01/
Feb/2020:17:45:14 +0000] "GET /\
 HTTP/1.1" 200 612 "-" "curl/7.58.0" "-"
[pod/nginx-86c57db685-5f73p/nginx] 127.0.0.1 - - [01/
Feb/2020:17:45:17 +0000] "GET /\
 HTTP/1.1" 200 612 "-" "curl/7.58.0" "-"
```

The other available flags for the `logs` command are as follows:

- `--follow` (`-f` for short) allows to **follow** the stream; use Ctrl-C to stop.

- `--previous` (`-p` for short) allows to view the logs of the **previous** containers, which is useful when a container crashed and you want to see the error that made it crash.

- `--container=name` (`-c name` for short) shows the logs of a specific container, and `--all-containers` shows the logs of all the containers.

- `--timestamps` displays timestamps of logs at the beginning of lines.

Logging at the Node Level

By default, the logs of a Pod are stored in the node running the Pod. When you are deploying the cluster with `kubeadm`, the logs can be found in the `/var/log/pods` directory. It is the responsibility of the cluster administrator to install some log rotation for these logs.

Cluster-Level Logging with a Node Logging Agent

Logs collected at the node level can be exported to an external logging backend (`syslog`, `StackDriver`, `Elastic`, etc.). `fluentd` (`www.fluentd.org`) is a logging agent that you can deploy on each node that will collect the logs and send them to the logging backend. You can deploy `fluentd` using a `DaemonSet` or a dedicated service on the node system.

Using a Sidecar to Redirect Logs to stdout

If your application is not able to output logs to stdout or stderr, but only to files, you can run a sidecar container that will read these log files and stream them to its own stdout. This way, the logs become available at the node level and can be explored with kubectl logs and exported with a logging agent.

Monitoring

You can use the kubectl top command to monitor the nodes of the clusters and the Pods.

To use this command, you first have to install the **Metrics Server** on your cluster. You can follow the instructions in Chapter 7 to install it.

Then, you can run the following commands to get the CPU and memory usage for each node and Pod:

```
$ kubectl top nodes
NAME          CPU(cores)   CPU%   MEMORY(bytes)   MEMORY%
controller    180m         18%    1391Mi          38%
worker-0      83m          8%     1294Mi          36%

$ kubectl top pods
NAME                        CPU(cores)   MEMORY(bytes)
nginx-d9bc977d8-2bf2g       0m           2Mi
```

The Metrics Server and the kubectl top command only give you a limited set of short-term metrics. It is recommended to install a complete monitoring solution.

Monitoring with Prometheus

Prometheus (prometheus.io) is a complete monitoring and alerting solution graduated by the CNCF. The Prometheus system is mainly composed of

- A server which scrapes and stores time series data

- Client libraries for instrumenting application code

- A node exporter to export host metrics

- An alert manager to handle alerts

The server, a stateful application, will regularly pull nodes and application components to scrape time series data containing metrics to monitor and save this data to its database.

Application developers are responsible for exposing metrics to monitor with the help of client libraries provided by Prometheus. The metrics are generally exposed on the `/metrics` endpoint.

Cluster administrators are responsible for deploying node exporters on the cluster nodes that will automatically expose the metrics of the host.

An alert manager is used to create and configure alarms based on one or more collected metrics.

The **Grafana** dashboard (`www.grafana.com`) is the Prometheus companion that will help you graphically expose and explore your metrics.

CHAPTER 15

Upgrading the Cluster

Upgrading the Kubernetes cluster is done in two phases. You first upgrade the control plane nodes and then the worker nodes. It is possible to upgrade to the next minor release or to any other next patch release of the same minor release. For example, when your cluster is using the version 1.18.6, you could upgrade to 1.18.p where p >= 7 and to 1.19.x (whatever the value of x), but not to 1.20.x.

As the control plane and workers are running on host systems, you will also need to upgrade these systems. You will see how to prepare the cluster to make these operations without interrupting your applications.

Finally, you will see how to back up and restore your cluster certificates and data.

Upgrade the Controller

First, install the desired version of kubeadm:

```
$ gcloud compute ssh controller
Welcome to controller
$ sudo apt update && apt-cache policy kubeadm
$ sudo apt update && \
   sudo apt-get install \
   -y --allow-change-held-packages \
   kubeadm=1.19.0-00
```

© Philippe Martin 2021
P. Martin, *Kubernetes*, https://doi.org/10.1007/978-1-4842-6494-2_15

```
$ sudo apt-mark hold kubeadm
$ kubeadm version -o short
v1.19.0
```

Drain the controller node:

```
$ kubectl drain controller --ignore-daemonsets \
  --delete-local-data
node/controller evicted
```

Check the possible upgrade plans:

```
$ sudo kubeadm upgrade plan
```

```
[...]
```

```
Components that must be upgraded manually after you have
upgraded the control plane \
with 'kubeadm upgrade apply':
COMPONENT    CURRENT       AVAILABLE
Kubelet      3 x v1.18.6   v1.19.0
```

```
Upgrade to the latest stable version:
```

COMPONENT	CURRENT	AVAILABLE
API Server	v1.18.6	v1.19.0
Controller Manager	v1.18.6	v1.19.0
Scheduler	v1.18.6	v1.19.0
Kube Proxy	v1.18.6	v1.19.0
CoreDNS	1.6.7	1.6.7
Etcd	3.4.3	3.4.3-0

```
You can now apply the upgrade by executing the following command:

        kubeadm upgrade apply v1.19.0
```

Several possibilities are displayed: one to upgrade to the latest version of the series and another one to upgrade to the latest stable version available with the version of kubeadm used.

In the preceding screen is displayed only the plan to upgrade to the latest stable version.

Let's start the upgrade:

```
$ sudo kubeadm upgrade apply v1.19.0
[...]
[upgrade/successful] SUCCESS! Your cluster was upgraded to "v1.19.0".
Enjoy!
```

Make the node schedulable again:

```
$ kubectl uncordon controller
node/controller uncordoned
```

Upgrade kubelet and kubectl on the controller:

```
$ sudo apt-get update && \
  sudo apt-get install \
  -y --allow-change-held-packages \
  kubelet=1.19.0-00 kubectl=1.19.0-00
$ sudo apt-mark hold kubelet kubectl
```

At this point, the controller node should show the latest version:

```
$ kubectl get nodes
NAME         STATUS   ROLES     AGE   VERSION
controller   Ready    master    13d   v1.19.0
worker-0     Ready    <none>    13d   v1.18.6
worker-1     Ready    <none>    13d   v1.18.6
```

Upgrade the Workers

Repeat these steps for each worker.

First, drain the node, from your machine:

```
$ kubectl drain worker-0 --ignore-daemonsets
node/worker-0 cordoned
node/worker-0  drained
```

Then, connect to the node and install the desired version of kubeadm:

```
$ gcloud compute ssh worker-0
Welcome to worker-0
$ sudo apt update && \
   sudo apt-get install \
   -y --allow-change-held-packages \
   kubeadm=1.19.0-00
$ sudo apt-mark hold kubeadm
$ kubeadm version -o short
v1.19.0
```

Upgrade the node:

```
$ sudo kubeadm upgrade node
[...]
[upgrade] The configuration for this node was successfully updated!
```

Upgrade kubelet and kubectl on the node:

```
$ sudo apt-get update && \
   sudo apt-get install \
   -y --allow-change-held-packages \
   kubelet=1.19.0-00 kubectl=1.19.0-00
$ sudo apt-mark hold kubelet kubectl
```

From your machine, make the node schedulable again:

```
$ kubectl uncordon worker-0
node/worker-0 uncordoned
```

After upgrading all worker nodes, you should obtain the latest release on each node of the cluster:

```
$ kubectl get nodes
NAME         STATUS   ROLES    AGE   VERSION
controller   Ready    master   13d   v1.19.0
worker-0     Ready    <none>   13d   v1.19.0
worker-1     Ready    <none>   13d   v1.19.0
```

Upgrading the Operating System

If you need to reboot the host of a cluster node for maintenance (e.g., for a kernel or hardware upgrade), you first need to **drain** the node:

```
$ kubectl drain $NODENAME --ignore-daemonsets
node/nodename drained
```

Draining the node will have two effects:

- Evict all Pods from this node, all Pods controlled by a ReplicaSet being rescheduled on another node.

- Make this node unschedulable, so that no new Pod is scheduled on this node during the maintenance.

You can now safely make maintenance operations on the operating system or hardware.

Once the maintenance is over, you can **uncordon** the node, to make the node schedulable again:

```
$ kubectl uncordon $NODENAME
node/nodename uncordoned
```

Back Up a Cluster

Back up the files /etc/kubernetes/pki/ca.crt and /etc/kubernetes/
pki/ca.key after cluster installation.

Periodically create a snapshot of the etcd database with the command

```
$ kubectl exec -it -n kube-system etcd-controller \
    sh -- -c "ETCDCTL_API=3 etcdctl snapshot save snapshot.db \
    --cacert /etc/kubernetes/pki/etcd/server.crt \
    --cert /etc/kubernetes/pki/etcd/ca.crt \
    --key /etc/kubernetes/pki/etcd/ca.key"
Snapshot saved at snapshot.db
$ kubectl cp -n kube-system etcd-controller:snapshot.db snapshot.db
```

Restore a Cluster

Install the controller again by following the steps in Chapter 1 and stop
before running kubeadm init.

Copy ca.crt and ca.key in /etc/kubernetes/pki, restoring the good
permissions:

```
# ls -l /etc/kubernetes/pki/
total  8
-rw-r--r-- 1 root root 1025 Feb 1 10:43 ca.crt
-rw------- 1 root root 1675 Feb 1 10:43 ca.key
```

Place snapshot.db in /mnt and then run:

```
$ docker run --rm \
    -v '/mnt:/backup' \
    -v '/var/lib/etcd:/var/lib/etcd' \
    --env ETCDCTL_API=3 \
    'k8s.gcr.io/etcd-amd64:3.1.12' \
```

```
/bin/sh -c \
"etcdctl snapshot restore /backup/snapshot.db ; mv /default.
etcd/member/ /var/lib/etcd/"
```

Install the control plane again:

```
$ gcloud config set compute/zone us-west1-c # or your selected
zone
Updated property [compute/zone].
$ KUBERNETES_PUBLIC_ADDRESS=$(gcloud compute instances describe
controller \
  --zone $(gcloud config get-value compute/zone) \
  --format='get(networkInterfaces[0].accessConfigs[0].natIP)')
$ sudo kubeadm init \
  --pod-network-cidr=10.244.0.0/16 \
  --ignore-preflight-errors=NumCPU \
  --apiserver-cert-extra-sans=$KUBERNETES_PUBLIC_ADDRESS \
  --ignore-preflight-errors=DirAvailable--var-lib-etcd
```

CHAPTER 16

Command-Line Tools

kubectl

kubectl is the command-line tool used to work on Kubernetes clusters. You can use it to create application resources and cluster resources, interact with running containers, and manage the cluster.

kubectl completion

This command outputs the shell code to execute to make the auto-completion work with the kubectl command. Its simplest usage is to "*source*" its output that will make auto-completion available for the current shell session:

```
$ source <(kubectl completion bash)
```

or, if using the zsh shell:

```
$ source <(kubectl completion zsh)
```

Run kubectl completion --help to get the instructions on how to install the completion in a permanent way.

© Philippe Martin 2021
P. Martin, *Kubernetes*, https://doi.org/10.1007/978-1-4842-6494-2_16

Managing the kubeconfig File

kubectl and other Kubernetes programs get the credentials necessary to connect to Kubernetes clusters in a *kubeconfig* file. This file is by default searched at $HOME/.kube/config. It is possible to use another file either by using the --kubeconfig flag or by defining the KUBECONFIG environment variable.

The value of KUBECONFIG is a colon-delimited list of paths to config files, for example:

```
/etc/kubernetes/config:$HOME/.kube/config
```

When defining several paths, kubectl will **merge** these different files (in memory) and use the results as a single config file.

A kubeconfig file is composed of

- A **list of cluster information** (certificate, API URL)

- A **list of user credentials**

- A **list of contexts**, each context referencing existing *cluster, user, and default namespace*

- A **current context**, pointing to a specific context in the list of contexts

kubectl config

> This command provides subcommands to edit the list of clusters, users, and contexts and to switch the current context:

- get-clusters, set-cluster, delete-cluster to edit cluster information.

- set-credentials to edit user credentials.

- `get-contexts`, `set-context`, `delete-context`, `rename-context` to edit contexts.

- `set` and `unset` are generic subcommands to edit any field of the kubeconfig file.

- `current-context` to get the name of the current context.

- `use-context` to set the name of the current context.

- `view` to view the kubeconfig information visible by the command (depending on the `--kubeconfig` flag and `KUBECONFIG` environment variable), especially useful to see the result of merging several config files or getting the information necessary for the current context with `--minify`.

Generic Commands

kubectl apply

Most kubectl commands are used in *imperative* mode. The `apply` command is on the contrary used in *declarative* mode, for *applying* YAML/JSON templates, that is, for declaring resources to the cluster API based on their definitions in YAML or JSON files.

kubectl get

Get a tabular list of resources or their complete definitions with the `-o yaml` flag.

kubectl delete

Delete a resource or a set of resources.

195

kubectl edit

Interactively edit a resource definition in your preferred editor (you can change the EDITOR environment variable to change it).

kubectl create namespace

Create a new namespace.

Creating Application Resources

Creating and Parameterizing Workloads

kubectl run

Deploy a new workload. Most forms of these commands are deprecated.

The one not deprecated is to deploy a Pod with a single container:

kubectl run podname --image=imagename

Flags are available to set specific fields of the container: image pull policy, environment variables, ports, resource requests, and limits.

The dry-run=client -o yaml is useful to output the declarative form of the Pod that can be edited and applied later with kubectl apply.

kubectl create deployment

Create a Deployment in its simplest form: kubectl create deployment nginx --image=nginx. No flags are available to parameterize the Deployment.

The `dry-run=client -o yaml` is useful to output the declarative form of the Deployment that can be edited and applied later with `kubectl apply`.

The `set` and `scale` commands are useful to parameterize the Deployment.

kubectl create cronjob

Create a cronjob, given an image and a schedule. You can also specify the command and args to pass to the container, useful when using a generic image like busybox:

```
kubectl create cronjob pinghost --image=busybox \
--schedule="10 * * * *" \
-- sh -c 'ping -c 1 myhost'
```

Use `man 5 crontab` to get the specifications of the schedule flag.

The `dry-run=client -o yaml` is useful to output the declarative form of the cronjob that can be edited and applied later with `kubectl apply`.

kubectl create job

Execute a job. Two forms are available:

- Create a job given an image and optionally a command (very similar to the `create cronjob` command but for a single job):

```
kubectl create job pinghost --image=busybox \
-- sh -c 'ping -c 1 myhost'
```

- Create a job from an existing cronjob, bypassing the cronjob's schedule:

```
kubectl create job pinghost --from=cronjob/pinghost
```

kubectl scale

Scale applicable resources (Deployment, ReplicaSet, StatefulSet) to the given number of replicas. The selection of the resources to scale is done by type/name, label selector, or file. Some preconditions can be specified: number of current replicas and version of the resource.

kubectl autoscale

Create an auto-scaler for applicable resources (Deployment, ReplicaSet, StatefulSet). The selection of the resources to auto-scale is done by type/name or file. The important flags are `min`, `max`, and `cpu-percent` to indicate the limits in number of replicas and the **average** CPU percentage at which the resource will be scaled.

kubectl rollout

Set of commands for rolling update and rollback of applicable resources (Deployment, DaemonSet, StatefulSet). See section "Update and Rollback" in Chapter 5 for details.

Configuring Workloads

kubectl create configmap

Create a `ConfigMap` resource, getting key/value pairs:

- From env-style files (`--from-env-file`): The keys and values will be extracted from the file

```
# .env
key1=value1
key2=value2
```

- From files (`--from-file`): The key will be the filename or the specified key and the value the contents of the file, for the specified file or all files of the specified directory:

```
--from-file=dir --from-file=file1.txt --from-
file=key=file2.txt
```

- From literal values (`--from-literal`):

```
--from-literal=key1=value1 --from-literal=key2=value2
```

kubectl create secret

Create a `Secret` resource. Three forms are available:

- `create secret generic`: Very similar to `create configmap`, to add key/value pairs from env-style files, files and literal values.

- `create secret docker-registry`: Create a Secret to be used as an `imagePullSecrets` (see section "Working with Private Docker Registries" in Chapter 11). Two forms are available, from a Docker config file (`--from-file`) or by specifying registry information (`--docker-server`, `--docker-username`, `--docker-password`, and `--docker-email`).

- `create secret tls`: Create a TLS secret given a public/private key pair (`--cert` and `--key`) stored in files.

Exposing Pods

`kubectl create service`

Create a `Service` resource. Four forms are available, one for each Service type:

- `create service clusterip` creates a ClusterIP Service, specifying the ports with the `--tcp` flag:

  ```
  kubectl create service clusterip my-svc \
  --tcp=8084:80
  ```

  A selector `app=my-svc` will be added, to match Pods with this label. You will probably need to edit it to match the labels of the desired Pods.

  It is possible to specify your own IP for the Service with `--clusterip=x.y.z.a` or create a Headless Service with `--clusterip=None`.

- `create service nodeport` creates a NodePort Service. In addition to the `clusterip` variant, it is possible to specify a node port with the `--node-port` flag:

  ```
  kubectl create service nodeport my-svc \
  --tcp=8084:80 --node-port=30080
  ```

- `create service loadbalancer` creates a LoadBalancer Service, specifying the clusterIP ports with the `--tcp` flag:

  ```
  kubectl create service loadbalancer my-svc \
  --tcp=8084:80
  ```

  Note that it is not possible to specify a port for the underlying node port.

- create service externalname creates an
  ExternalName Service:

  ```
  kubectl create service externalname my-svc \
  --external-name=an-svc.domain.com
  ```

kubectl expose

Expose an applicable resource (Service, Pod,
ReplicaSet, Deployment) creating a new Service
resource.

Authorization

kubectl create role
   kubectl create clusterrole
   kubectl create rolebinding
   kubectl create clusterrolebinding
   kubectl create serviceaccount
   kubectl auth
All these commands are used to create and verify authorizations. See
section "Authorization" in Chapter 11 for details.

Annotate and Label

kubectl annotate

Attach metadata to any kind of resource, not used
by Kubernetes but intended to be used by tools or
system extensions.

kubectl label

Edit labels on any kind of resource, used as selectors.

Interacting with the Application

kubectl attach

> Attach to a process already running inside an existing container and show its output.

kubectl exec

> Execute a new command into an existing container.

kubectl cp

> Copy files from/to an existing container to/from your local computer.

The syntax of the source and destination files are

- `/path/to/file` for a file in your local computer

- `pod:/path/to/file` for a file in the container of pod

- `namespace/pod:/path/to/file` for a file in pod container in `namespace`

The `-c container` flag indicates which specific container of the Pod is targetedv.

kubectl describe

> Display the details of a resource.

kubectl logs

> Print the logs for a container in a Pod.

kubectl port-forward

> Forward local ports to a Pod:

> `kubectl port-forward type/name local-port:remote-port`

type can be a Pod, a workload managing a Pod
(ReplicaSet, Deployment, etc.), or a Service
exposing a Pod.

The `--address ip` flag specifies the local address to
listen on, `127.0.0.1` by default.

kubectl proxy

Run a proxy on your local machine to the
Kubernetes API server.

kubectl top

Display resource (CPU/memory/storage) usage for
nodes or Pods.

Managing Clusters

kubectl taint

Edit taints of nodes.

kubectl uncordon

Mark a node as schedulable.

kubectl cordon

Mark a node as unschedulable.

kubectl drain

Prepare a node for maintenance by marking it as
unschedulable and evicting Pods from this node.

kubectl certificate

Approve/deny a certificate signing request.

kubectl cluster-info

> Display the addresses of the master and services. The dump subcommand dumps all information suitable for debugging and diagnosing cluster problems.

kubectl version

> Display the version of client and server.

Getting Documentation

kubectl api-versions

> Display the supported API versions on the server.

kubectl api-resources

> Display the supported API resources on the server.

kubectl explain

> List and document fields of a resource.

kubectl options

> Display the generic flags supported by all commands.

kubectl help

> Display inline help about kubectl.

Helm

Helm is a package manager for Kubernetes.

Helm charts are packages that help you define, install, and upgrade Kubernetes applications, and these charts are stored in Helm repositories.

You can use the helm command to search, install, upgrade, roll back, and uninstall charts.

Install Helm on Your dev Machine

Helm consists of a single binary, helm. You can install it either by manually downloading this binary or by using the package manager of your system. The following are the instructions to download and install the binary for different operating systems.

You can get the latest releases at https://github.com/helm/helm/releases.

Linux

```
$ curl -LO https://get.helm.sh/helm-v3.3.0-linux-amd64.tar.gz
$ tar zxvf helm-v3.3.0-linux-amd64.tar.gz
$ sudo mv ./linux-amd64/helm /usr/local/bin/helm
# Test it is working correctly
$ helm version --short
v3.3.0+g8a4aeec
```

macOS

```
$ curl -LO https://get.helm.sh/helm-v3.3.0-darwin-amd64.tar.gz
$ tar zxvf helm-v3.3.0-linux-amd64.tar.gz
$ sudo mv ./linux-amd64/helm /usr/local/bin/helm
# Test it is working correctly
$ helm version --short
v3.3.0+g8a4aeec
```

Windows

```
$ url -LO https://get.helm.sh/helm-v3.3.0-windows-amd64.zip
# Unzip the downloaded file,
# Move the helm binary into your PATH,
$ helm version --short
v3.3.0+g8a4aeec
```

Install Charts

The charts are stored in Helm repositories. You can use the Helm Hub
(https://hub.helm.sh/) to discover new repositories.

The helm repo command helps you manage the repositories you have
access to. After installation, you can see that you do not have access to any
repository:

```
$ helm repo list
Error: no repositories to show
```

You can add a new repository with the command helm repo add, for
example:

```
$ helm repo add bitnami https://charts.bitnami.com/bitnami
"bitnami" has been added to your repositories
$ helm repo list
NAME      URL
Bitnami   https://charts.bitnami.com/bitnami
```

Now, you can install a chart from this repository:

```
$ helm install my-wp-install bitnami/wordpress
[...]
```

Later, when a new version is released, you can upgrade your
installation with the helm upgrade command:

```
$ helm upgrade my-wp-install bitnami/wordpress
Release "my-wp-install" has been upgraded. Happy Helming!
[...]
```

You can manage the history of the deployed revisions with helm history:

```
$ helm history my-wp-install
REVISION  UPDATED                     STATUS
    CHART                 APP VERSION  DESCRIPTION
1         Sat Aug 10 10:39:04 2020    superseded
    wordpress-9.4.2     .4.1          Install complete
2         Sat Aug 15 10:46:54 2020    deployed
      wordpress-9.4.3  5.4.2          Upgrade complete
```

If necessary, you can roll back to a previous release:

```
$ helm rollback my-wp-install 1
Rollback was a success! Happy Helming!
$ helm history my-wp-install
REVISION  UPDATED                     STATUS
    CHART                 APP VERSION  DESCRIPTION
1         Sat Aug 10 10:39:04 2020    superseded
    wordpress-9.4.2     5.4.1         Install complete
2         Sat Aug 15 10:46:54 2020    superseded
    wordpress-9.4.3     5.4.2         Upgrade complete
3         Sat Aug 15 10:50:59 2020    deployed
    wordpress-9.4.2     5.4.1         Rollback to 1
```

You can uninstall the package with the `helm uninstall` command:

```
$ helm uninstall my-wp-install
release "my-wp-install" uninstalled
```

Create Your Own Charts

The command `helm create` is used to create your own package. When you run this command, it will create for you a new directory structure with a default application:

```
$ helm create my-nginx
Creating my-nginx
$ tree my-nginx
my-nginx
├── charts
├── Chart.yaml
├── templates
│   ├── deployment.yaml
│   ├── _helpers.tpl
│   ├── hpa.yaml
│   ├── ingress.yaml
│   ├── NOTES.txt
│   ├── serviceaccount.yaml
│   ├── service.yaml
│   └── tests
│       └── test-connection.yaml
└── values.yaml
```

The `Chart.yaml` file contains metadata about the package.

The `templates` directory contains the Kubernetes manifests that will be used to deploy the different resources that compose your application (a Deployment, a Service, an Ingress, a ServiceAccount, and a Horizontal Pod Autoscaler). If you look at one of these files, you can see that these manifests are templated.

The `values.yaml` file contains the values used to personalize the final manifests that will be created by the templates.

Helm uses the Go templates engine, and you can find all the details about the associated language at `https://helm.sh/docs/chart_template_guide/`.

You are free to delete the files in the `templates` directory and the `values.yaml` and create your own templates and values files, or edit them if your application is similar to the default one.

When you have finished editing the templates and values, you can package your chart with the command `helm package`:

```
$ helm package my-nginx/
Successfully packaged chart and saved it to: my-nginx-0.1.0.tgz
```

This command creates an archive file containing your templates. You can either distribute this chart through a Helm repository or use it locally, with the command

```
$ helm install test-my-nginx ./my-nginx-0.1.0.tgz
[...]
```

Kustomize

Unlike Helm which is based on templates, Kustomize is based on customization.

This tool is useful when you want to reuse the manifests to deploy an application in a limited number of environments.

For this, you first define *base* manifests that contain the common base for all the environments; then you create *overlays* to specialize the base manifests for each environment, by applying *patches* and *transformers* to these base manifests.

Dev and Production Environments Example

For this typical case, we will create a base directory that will contain
the base manifests common to both environments and then dev and
production directories that will be used to deploy to, respectively, dev and
production environments.

We will create the following structure of files:

```
$ tree .
.
├── base
│   ├── deployment.yaml
│   ├── kustomization.yaml
│   └── service.yaml
├── dev
│   ├── kustomization.yaml
│   ├── namespace.yaml
│   └── resources-patch.yaml
└── production
    ├── kustomization.yaml
    ├── namespace.yaml
    └── resources-patch.yaml

// base/deployment.yaml
apiVersion: apps/v1
kind: Deployment
metadata:
  labels:
    app: nginx
  name: nginx
spec:
  selector:
```

```
    matchLabels:
      app: nginx
  template:
    metadata:
      labels:
        app: nginx
    spec:
      containers:
      - image: nginx
        name: nginx

// base/service.yaml
apiVersion: v1
kind:   Service
metadata:
  labels:
    app: nginx
  name: nginx
spec:
  ports:
  - name: http
    port: 80
    protocol: TCP
    targetPort: 80
  selector:
    app: nginx
  type: ClusterIP

// base/kustomization.yaml
resources:
- deployment.yaml
- service.yaml
```

From the base directory, you can use the following command:

```
$ cd base
$ kubectl apply -k .
service/nginx created
deployment.apps/nginx created
# clean
$ kubectl delete -k .
```

When using kubectl apply with the -k flag, the command will look at a kustomization.yaml file into the directory specified in the command line (here the current directory) and will apply it.

A kustomization.yaml file contains directives of different types:

- The resources directive that points to manifest files

- The *patches* directives that will apply specified patches to these manifests

- The *modifiers* directives that will modify in some specific ways these manifests.

So, when the kubectl *applies* a directory containing a kustomization. yaml file, it will first load the resources, then patch and modify them, and finally apply the resulting manifests as the kubectl apply -f command would do.

Back to our example, the kustomization.yaml file only contains a resources directive; it is then equivalent to applying the two files deployment.yaml and service.yaml.

We will now create an overlay for the dev environment. Here is the kustomization and associated files:

```
// dev/kustomization.yaml
bases:
- ../base/
```

```
resources:
- namespace.yaml

namespace: dev

commonLabels:
  env: dev

patchesStrategicMerge:
- resources-patch.yaml

// dev/namespace.yaml
kind: Namespace
metadata:
  name: dev

// dev/resources-patch.yaml
apiVersion: apps/v1
kind: Deployment
metadata:
  name: nginx
spec:
  template:
    spec:
      containers:
      - name: nginx
        resources:
          requests:
            cpu: 100m
            memory: 100Mi
```

In the kustomization.yaml file, the bases directive indicates that this
overlay is based on the kustomization file in the ../base directory.

Then some new resource is included: here the manifest to create the dev namespace.

Next, some modifiers are applied: `namespace` will modify each resource manifest to set the `metadata.namespace` value as dev, and `commonLabels` will add the `env: dev` label to each resource manifest.

Finally, the patch found in `resources-patch.yaml` will be applied, to add resource requests to the Deployment.

Some other modifiers are available, including the following:

- `namePrefix` and `nameSuffix` will modify the `metadata.name` of each resource manifest with the given prefix or suffix.

- `commonAnnotations` will add annotations to each resource manifest.

- `images` is a mapping of old/new image names that will change the values of container image names found in manifests.

- `replicas` will change the replica count of each concerned resource manifest.

As an exercise, you can create the overlay for the production environment with specific patches and modifiers for the production.

Rolling Configuration Update

The two directives `configMapGenerator` and `secretGenerator` are used to generate ConfigMaps and Secrets from the `kustomization.yaml` file.

When these generators create a ConfigMap or Secret, they add a random suffix to its name, and the reference from a container to this resource is modified to include this suffix. This way, when you update a generated ConfigMap or Secret, a new one is created and, more

interestingly, the Deployment referencing this resource is updated to
change the configmap/secret name; new Pods will be launched through a
rolling update to apply this new configuration.

As an example, here are manifests for an nginx container serving static
files from a ConfigMap:

```
// deployment.yaml
apiVersion: apps/v1
kind: Deployment
metadata:
  labels:
    app: nginx
  name: nginx
spec:
  selector:
    matchLabels:
      app: nginx
  template:
    metadata:
      labels:
        app: nginx
    spec:
      volumes:
      - name: static-files
        configMap:
          name: static-files
      containers:
      - image: nginx
        name: nginx
        volumeMounts:
        - mountPath: /usr/share/nginx/html
          name: static-files
```

```
<!-- index.html -->
version 1
```

```
// kustomization.yaml
resources:
- deployment.yaml
```

```
configMapGenerator:
- name: static-files
  files:
  - index.html
```

Let's apply these manifests with Kustomize:

```
$ kubectl apply -k .
configmap/static-files-ck2b6hc6th created
deployment.apps/nginx created
```

We can see that the created ConfigMap is named `static-files-ck2b6hc6th`, when we named it `static-files` in the `configMapGenerator` directive. Also, we can see that the ConfigMap referenced in the PodTemplate of the Deployment is also `static-files-ck2b6hc6th` and not `static-files` as specified:

```
$ kubectl get deployments.apps nginx -o jsonpath='{.spec.
template.spec.volumes[0].configMap.name}'
static-files-ck2b6hc6th
```

Now, edit the index.html file, and then apply the `kustomization.yaml` file again:

```
$ echo 'version 2' > index.html
$ kubectl apply -k .
configmap/static-files-bg9hg69mh9 created
deployment.apps/nginx configured
```

```
$ kubectl get deployments.apps nginx -o jsonpath='{.spec.
template.spec.volumes[0].configMap.name}'
static-files-bg9hg69mh9

$ kubectl rollout history deployment nginx
deployment.apps/nginx
REVISION   CHANGE-CAUSE
1          <none>
2          <none>
```

You can see that a new ConfigMap named static-files-bg9hg69mh9 has been created, the Deployment has been updated to reference this new ConfigMap, and a rollout of the Deployment occurred.

Note that you can disable this behavior by using the disableNameSuffixHash option:

```
[...]
configMapGenerator:
- name: static-files
  files:
  - index.html
  options:
    disableNameSuffixHash: true
```

APPENDIX A

Curriculum CKA 1.19: September 2020

Cluster Architecture, Installation, and Configuration (25%)

Manage role-based access control (RBAC).

"Authorization," Chapter 11

Use kubeadm to install a basic cluster.

Chapter 1

Manage a highly available Kubernetes cluster.

Chapter 1

Provision underlying infrastructure to deploy a Kubernetes cluster.

Chapter 1

Perform a version upgrade on a Kubernetes cluster using kubeadm.

Chapter 15

Implement etcd backup and restore.

"Back Up a Cluster," "Restore a Cluster," Chapter 15

© Philippe Martin 2021
P. Martin, *Kubernetes*, https://doi.org/10.1007/978-1-4842-6494-2

Workloads and Scheduling (15%)

Understand deployments and how to perform rolling update and rollbacks.

"ReplicaSet Controller," "Deployment Controller," "Update and Rollback," and "Deployment Strategies," Chapter 5

Use ConfigMaps and Secrets to configure applications.

Chapter 6

Know how to scale applications.

Chapter 7

Understand the primitives used to create robust, self-healing, application deployments.

Chapter 8

Understand how resource limits can affect Pod scheduling.

"Resource Requests," Chapter 9

Awareness of manifest management and common templating tools.

"Helm," "Kustomize," Chapter 16

Services and Networking (20%)

Understand host networking configuration on the cluster nodes.

Chapter 1

Understand connectivity between Pods.

Chapter 1

Understand ClusterIP, NodePort, and LoadBalancer service types and endpoints.

Chapter 10

Know how to use Ingress controllers and Ingress resources.

Chapter 10

Know how to configure and use CoreDNS.

Chapter 1

Choose an appropriate container network interface plugin.

Chapter 1

Storage (10%)

Understand storage classes and persistent volumes.

Chapter 12

Understand volume mode, access modes, and reclaim policies for volumes.

"Access Modes," "Claiming a Persistent Volume," Chapter 12

Understand persistent volume claims primitive.

"Claiming a Persistent Volume," Chapter 12

Know how to configure applications with persistent storage.

"Persistent Volume," Chapter 12

Troubleshooting (30%)

Evaluate cluster and node logging.

Chapter 2

Understand how to monitor applications.

"Auto-scaling," Chapter 7; "kubectl," Chapter 16

Manage container stdout and stderr logs.

Logging in the Chapter 14

Troubleshoot application failure.

Basic logging, "kubectl," Chapter 16

Troubleshoot cluster component failure.

Chapter 2

Troubleshoot networking.

Chapter 2, Chapter 10, "kubectl," Chapter 16

Curriculum CKAD 1.18: April 2020

Core Concepts (13%)

Understand Kubernetes API primitives.

Chapters 4 and 5

Create and configure basic Pods.

Chapter 5

Configuration (18%)

Understand ConfigMaps.

Chapter 6

Understand SecurityContexts.

"Security Contexts," Chapter 11

Define an application's resource requirements.

"Resource Requests," Chapter 9; "Resource Limits and Quality of Service (QoS) Classes," Chapter 8

Create and consume Secrets.

Chapter 6

Understand ServiceAccounts

"Service Account Authentication," Chapter 11

Multi-container Pods (10%)

Understand multi-container Pod design patterns (e.g., ambassador, adapter, sidecar).

Chapter 13

Observability (18%)

Understand LivenessProbes and ReadinessProbes.

"Liveness Probes," "A Note About Readiness Probes," Chapter 8; "Readiness Probes," Chapter 10

Understand container logging.

Basic logging

Understand how to monitor applications in Kubernetes.

"Auto-scaling," Chapter 7

Understand debugging in Kubernetes

"Interacting with the Application," Chapter 16

Pod Design (20%)

Understand Deployments and how to perform rolling updates.

"Update and Rollback," "Deployment Strategies," Chapter 5

Understand Deployments and how to perform rollbacks.

"Update and Rollback," Chapter 5

Understand jobs and cronjobs.

"Running Jobs," Chapter 5

Understand how to use Labels, Selectors, and Annotations.

"Labels and Selectors," "Annotations," Chapter 4; Service Selectors in Chapter 10, "Using Label Selectors to Schedule Pods on Specific Nodes," Chapter 9

Services and Networking (13%)

Understand Services.

Chapter 10

Demonstrate basic understanding of NetworkPolicies.

"Network Policies," Chapter 11

State Persistence (8%)

Understand PersistentVolumeClaims for storage.

"Persistent Volume," Chapter 12

Index

U

V, W, X, Y, Z